THINK THRICE, CODE ONCE

THE ART OF THOUGHTFUL DEVELOPMENT FOR SMARTER, FASTER, AND BETTER SOFTWARE

AMIT GUJRATHI

To the thinkers, the dreamers, and the builders—
This book is for those who pause to reflect,
who strive for excellence,
and who believe that thoughtful creation
can change the world.

To my family and friends,
for their unwavering support and encouragement.

And to every developer out there,
who dares to think thrice before they code once.

Contents

Foreword

In the fast-paced world of software development, where deadlines loom and the pressure to deliver quickly often overshadows the need for quality, it's easy to fall into the trap of rushing through the process. Many developers, myself included, have learned the hard way that speed without strategy can lead to chaos—bug-ridden code, missed deadlines, and frustrated clients. But what if there was a better way? What if we could approach development with intention, clarity, and purpose, creating software that not only works but also stands the test of time?

That's where this book, "Think Thrice, Code Once," comes in. It's not just a guide to writing better code—it's a philosophy, a mindset, and a call to action for developers everywhere. The author takes us on a journey through the principles of thoughtful development, showing us how to slow down just enough to think critically, plan effectively, and execute with precision. It's a refreshing antidote to the "move fast and break things" mentality that has dominated the tech industry for far too long.

What makes this book truly special is its practicality. The author doesn't just preach about the importance of thoughtful development; they provide actionable strategies, real-world examples, and relatable stories that bring the concepts to life. From planning and design thinking to clean coding practices and debugging, every chapter is packed with insights that will resonate with developers at all levels of experience.

But this book isn't just for developers. It's for anyone who values craftsmanship, collaboration, and continuous improvement. Whether you're a project manager, a designer, or a team leader, the lessons in this book will help you foster a culture of thoughtfulness and excellence in your work.

As I read through these pages, I was reminded of my own journey as a developer—the mistakes I've made, the lessons I've learned, and the moments of clarity that have shaped my career. This book captures those moments and distills them into a framework that's both accessible and inspiring. It's a reminder that great software isn't just written—it's crafted with care, intention, and a deep understanding of the problem it's meant to solve.

So, as you embark on this journey, I encourage you to embrace the principles of thoughtful development. Take the time to think thrice before you code once. Challenge yourself to plan, reflect, and grow. And most importantly, enjoy the process. Because at the end of the day, thoughtful development isn't just about building better software—it's about becoming a better developer, teammate, and problem solver.

This book is a gift to the development community, and I'm confident it will inspire a new generation of thoughtful coders. I'm honored to write this foreword and excited for you to discover the wisdom within these pages.

Happy coding....

Preface

In the world of software development, speed often takes precedence over strategy. Deadlines loom, clients demand results, and the pressure to deliver quickly can push even the most skilled developers into a cycle of rushed decisions and hasty coding. I've been there—staring at a screen late at night, debugging a mess of my own making, wondering how I got to this point. It's a familiar story for many developers, but it doesn't have to be this way.

This book, "Think Thrice, Code Once," is born out of my own experiences, both the successes and the failures. Over the years, I've learned that the key to building great software isn't just about writing code—it's about how you approach the entire process. It's about taking a step back, thinking critically, and planning thoughtfully before diving into the keyboard. It's about adopting a mindset that values quality over speed, clarity over chaos, and long-term success over short-term wins.

The idea of "thinking thrice" is simple but powerful. It's a reminder to pause and reflect at every stage of development: before you plan, before you code, and before you deliver. It's about asking the right questions, anticipating challenges, and making intentional decisions that lead to better outcomes. When you think thrice, you don't just code once—you code with confidence, purpose, and precision.

This book is for developers of all levels, from those just starting their journey to seasoned professionals looking to refine their craft. It's packed with practical advice, real-world examples, and actionable strategies that you can apply to your work immediately. But more than that, it's a guide to adopting a thoughtful mindset—one that will not only make you a better developer but also help you enjoy the process of creating software.

As you read through these pages, you'll meet developers like Raj and Priya, whose contrasting approaches to coding illustrate the importance of thoughtful development. You'll explore the three pillars of this philosophy—planning, execution, and reflection—and learn how to apply them to every stage of the software lifecycle. And you'll discover how to navigate challenges like feature creep, technical debt, and tight deadlines with clarity and confidence.

This book isn't about perfection. Mistakes are inevitable, and they're often where the best learning happens. Instead, it's about progress—about becoming more intentional, more efficient, and more effective in your work. It's about building software that not only works but also lasts, delights users, and makes a meaningful impact.

Whether you're a solo developer, part of a team, or leading a project, my hope is that this book will inspire you to think differently about your work. To slow down just enough to think thrice before you code once. To embrace the art of thoughtful development and discover the joy of creating software that truly matters.

Thank you for picking up this book. I'm excited to share this journey with you, and I hope it helps you as much as these lessons have helped me.

Let's get started.

Acknowledgements

This book would not have been possible without the support, guidance, and inspiration of many incredible people.

To my family and friends, thank you for your unwavering encouragement and belief in me throughout this journey.

To my mentors, colleagues, and the developer community, your insights, feedback, and shared experiences have shaped my understanding of thoughtful development and inspired much of what is written here.

To my readers, thank you for taking the time to explore these ideas. Your passion for growth and learning is what drives this work.

Finally, to everyone who has ever paused to think before they code—this book is for you.

Thank you all.

CHAPTER ONE

INTRODUCTION TO THOUGHTFUL DEVELOPMENT

Why Thoughtful Development Matters

When I think about the difference between good developers and great ones, it often comes down to one thing: thoughtfulness. Thoughtful development isn't just about writing clean code or following best practices—it's a mindset. It's the ability to step back, think critically about the problem you're solving, and make intentional decisions that will stand the test of time. It's about crafting software with care, not just for the immediate task at hand, but for the people who will use it, maintain it, and build on it in the future. I didn't always understand this. Early in my career, I was more focused on speed than quality. I thought the faster I could deliver a feature, the better. But it didn't take long for me to learn that hasty coding comes with a cost—and that cost can be far greater than the time you think you're saving.

I remember one of the first projects I worked on as a junior developer. It was a simple e-commerce website for a small business, and the client wanted it up and running as quickly as possible. I was eager to prove myself, so I dove right in. I didn't spend much time planning or thinking about the architecture—I just started coding. At first, everything seemed to be going well. I was making progress quickly, and the client was happy with the initial results. But as the project grew, so did the problems. Features that seemed straightforward became difficult to implement because the codebase was a mess. Bugs started popping up in places I didn't expect, and fixing them often broke something else. By the time we launched, the site was barely holding together, and I was exhausted from working late nights trying to patch things up. The client was frustrated, and I was left wondering where I had gone wrong.

Looking back, I realize that the problem wasn't my technical skills—it was my approach. I had been so focused on delivering quickly that I hadn't taken the time to think about the bigger picture. I hadn't considered how the code I was writing would scale, how it would be maintained, or how it would affect the user experience. That project taught me a hard but valuable lesson: coding without a plan is like building a house without a blueprint. You might get the walls up, but sooner or later, the whole thing is going to collapse.

The cost of hasty coding isn't just technical—it's emotional. I've seen developers burn out because they're constantly firefighting, trying to fix problems that could have been avoided with a little more thought upfront. I've been on teams where the stress of dealing with a poorly designed system created tension and frustration, making it harder for everyone to do their best work. And I've seen clients lose trust in developers because they delivered something that worked in the short term but fell apart over time. These experiences have shown me that thoughtful development isn't just a nice-to-have—it's essential for building software that lasts.

But what does it mean to be a thoughtful developer? For me, it starts with asking the right questions. What problem am I solving? Who will use this software, and what do they need? How will this code be maintained, and by whom? These questions might seem simple, but they can have a profound impact on the decisions you make. I remember working on a project where we were building a scheduling tool for a healthcare provider. At first, we thought the most important feature was the ability to book appointments quickly. But when we talked to the users—nurses and administrative staff—we realized that their biggest pain point wasn't booking appointments; it was managing cancellations and rescheduling. By taking the time to understand their needs, we were able to design a system that addressed their real problems, not just the ones we assumed they had. That project taught me that thoughtful development isn't just about writing code—it's about understanding the people you're building for.

Thoughtful development also means anticipating challenges and planning for the future. I've worked on projects where the team took the time to think through the architecture, document their decisions, and write tests to catch bugs early. These projects weren't always the fastest to get off the ground, but they were the ones that succeeded in the long run. One of the best examples of this was a project I worked on for a fintech startup. The team was building a platform for managing investments, and from the very beginning, they prioritized thoughtful development. They spent weeks planning the architecture, designing APIs, and writing detailed documentation. At the time, it felt like overkill—why spend so much time planning when we could be coding? But as the project grew, it became clear how valuable that upfront work was. New features were easy to add because the architecture was flexible. Bugs were rare because the code was well-tested. And when new developers joined the team, they were able to get up to speed quickly because everything was so well-documented. That project taught me that thoughtful development isn't about being slow—it's about being smart.

Of course, thoughtful development doesn't mean you'll never make mistakes. I've made plenty, and I've learned that the key is to treat them as opportunities to grow. On one project, I designed a database schema that seemed fine at first but turned out to be a bottleneck as the application scaled. Fixing it was a painful process, but it taught me the importance of thinking about scalability from the start. On another project, I wrote a piece of code that was so complex that even I struggled to understand it a few months later. That experience taught me the value of simplicity and the importance of writing code that's easy to read and maintain. These mistakes were frustrating at the time, but they've made me a better developer by teaching me to think more carefully about the decisions I make.

One of the most inspiring things about thoughtful development is seeing the impact it can have—not just on the software you build, but on the people you work with. I've been on teams where thoughtful development was the norm, and the difference was night and day. Instead of rushing to meet deadlines, we took the time to plan, collaborate, and learn from each other. Instead of blaming each other when things went wrong, we worked together to find solutions. And instead of feeling stressed and overwhelmed, we felt proud of the work we were doing. These teams weren't just more productive—they were more enjoyable to be a part of. They showed me that thoughtful development isn't just about writing better code—it's about creating a better environment for everyone involved.

I've also seen how thoughtful development can lead to success stories that go beyond the code. I once worked with a developer who was known for their meticulous approach to planning and design. At first, some people thought they were too slow, but over time, their work spoke for itself. They built systems that were not only reliable and scalable but also a joy to use. One of their projects—a data visualization tool for a marketing agency—became so successful that it was adopted by other teams within the company and eventually turned into a standalone product. That developer's thoughtful approach didn't just solve the immediate problem—it created opportunities for growth and innovation that no one had anticipated.

Looking back, I realize that thoughtful development isn't just a skill—it's a mindset. It's the belief that good software isn't just written—it's designed, planned, and crafted with care. It's the willingness to slow down, ask questions, and think critically about the work you're doing. And it's the understanding that the decisions you make today will shape the future of the software you build—and the people who use it. Thoughtful development isn't always easy, especially when you're under pressure to deliver quickly. But in my experience, it's always worth it. Because when you take the time to think before you code, you're not just building software—you're building something that lasts.

The Big Picture of the Software Lifecycle

When I first started working as a developer, I thought my job was simple: write code, make it work, and move on to the next task. I didn't think much about what happened before I started coding or what came after I handed my work off to the next person. But as I gained more experience, I began to see that software development is about so much more than just writing code. It's part of a larger process—a lifecycle—that starts with an idea and doesn't end until the software is deployed, maintained, and eventually retired. Understanding this big picture has been one of the most important lessons of my career, and it's helped me become not just a better developer, but a better collaborator and problem-solver.

Every piece of software starts with an idea. Sometimes it's a clear, well-defined vision, like a client who wants to build an app to streamline their business operations. Other times, it's more abstract, like a vague sense that "we need to improve our user experience." Regardless of where the idea comes from, the first step in the software lifecycle is turning that idea into a plan. I've been on projects where this step was rushed or skipped entirely, and the results were almost always disastrous. Without a clear plan, it's easy to lose sight of the goal, waste time on unnecessary features, or end up with a product that doesn't meet the user's needs.

I remember one project where we were tasked with building a customer relationship management (CRM) tool for a small business. The client had a general idea of what they wanted, but they hadn't thought through the details. Instead of taking the time to clarify their requirements, we jumped straight into development, assuming we could figure things out as we went. At first, everything seemed fine—we were making progress, and the client was excited to see the initial results. But as the project went on, it became clear that we had misunderstood some of their key needs. Features we thought were important turned out to be irrelevant, while critical functionality was missing entirely. By the time we realized our mistake, we had already invested weeks of work, and fixing it required a complete overhaul of the codebase. That experience taught me the importance of thoughtful planning and communication at the start of a project. Taking the time to ask questions, define goals, and create a roadmap might seem like a delay, but it can save you countless hours of frustration down the line.

Once the planning phase is complete, the next step is development. This is the part of the lifecycle that most developers are familiar with, but even here, it's easy to lose sight of the big picture. I've seen developers get so focused on their individual tasks that they forget how their work fits into the larger system. On one project, I was working on a feature for a mobile app that allowed users to upload photos. I was so focused on making the upload process fast and reliable that I didn't think about how the feature would interact with the rest of the app. It wasn't until we started testing that I realized my code was causing performance issues on the server, which affected other parts of the app. Fixing the problem required not just changes to my code, but also adjustments to the server architecture and database design. That experience taught me to always think about how my work fits into the bigger picture and to collaborate closely with other team members to ensure everything works together seamlessly.

One of the most important lessons I've learned about the development phase is the value of communication. Software development is rarely a solo endeavor—it's a team effort that involves developers, designers, testers, project managers, and other stakeholders. Each person has their own perspective and expertise, and the best results come from working together. I've been on teams where communication was poor, and it almost always led to problems. On one project, the designers created a beautiful user interface, but they didn't consult with the developers about the technical feasibility of their designs. As a result, we ended up with a design that was nearly impossible to implement within the constraints of the project. If we had communicated more effectively from the start, we could have avoided a lot of wasted time and frustration.

After the development phase comes testing and deployment. This is where the software is put through its paces to ensure it works as intended and meets the user's needs. I've learned the hard way that testing is not something you can afford to skimp on. On one project, we were under pressure to meet a tight deadline, so we rushed through the testing phase. At first, everything seemed fine, but once the software was deployed, users started reporting bugs that we hadn't caught. Fixing those bugs after deployment was far more time-consuming and expensive than it would have been to catch them during testing. That experience taught me the importance of testing early and often, and of creating a culture where quality is a priority at every stage of the lifecycle.

Deployment is often seen as the end of the software lifecycle, but in reality, it's just the beginning of a new phase: maintenance. Once the software is in the hands of users, new challenges and opportunities arise. Bugs need to be fixed, features need to be updated, and the software needs to adapt to changing requirements and technologies. I've worked on projects where the team treated deployment as the finish line, only to be caught off guard when users started requesting changes or reporting issues. On one project, we deployed a web application without setting up a proper system for monitoring and logging. When users started experiencing performance issues, we had no way to diagnose the problem, and it took us weeks to figure out what was going wrong. That experience taught me the importance of planning for maintenance and support from the very beginning of a project.

Throughout the software lifecycle, there are many stakeholders involved, each with their own roles and responsibilities. Understanding these roles is crucial for effective collaboration and decision-making. I've worked on projects where the roles were unclear, and it almost always led to confusion and conflict. On one project, the client kept changing their requirements, and the project manager didn't step in to manage expectations. As a result, the developers were constantly scrambling to make changes, and the project fell behind schedule. That experience taught me the importance of having clear roles and responsibilities, and of working together to ensure everyone is aligned on the goals and priorities of the project.

One of the most common pitfalls in the software lifecycle is failing to involve the right stakeholders at the right time. I've seen projects where developers started building features without consulting the users who would actually be using them, only to discover later that the features didn't meet their needs. On one project, we were building a tool for data analysis, and we assumed that the users would want a lot of advanced features and customization options. But when we finally talked to the users, we discovered that they just wanted something simple and easy to use. If we had involved them earlier in the process, we could have saved a lot of time and effort.

Another common pitfall is underestimating the importance of documentation. I'll admit, I used to think documentation was boring and unnecessary. But after working on a project where the original developers left without documenting their work, I've come to appreciate its value. Trying to understand and maintain someone else's code without documentation is like trying to navigate a foreign city without a map—it's frustrating, time-consuming, and often leads to mistakes. That experience taught me that documentation isn't just for other people—it's for your future self, and for anyone who might work on the project after you.

Looking back, I've come to see the software lifecycle as a journey, with each stage building on the one before it. From idea to deployment, every step is an opportunity to learn, collaborate, and create something meaningful. By understanding the big picture and being thoughtful about each stage of the process, we can avoid common pitfalls, build better software, and create a more positive experience for everyone involved. Thoughtful development isn't just about writing good code—it's about seeing the whole picture and making decisions that lead to success at every stage of the lifecycle.

Overview of the Book's Framework

When I first started thinking about what it means to be a thoughtful developer, I struggled to put it into words. I knew it wasn't just about writing clean code or following best practices—those are important, of course, but they're only part of the picture. Thoughtful development is about something deeper. It's about the mindset you bring to your work, the way you approach problems, and the care you put into every decision. Over the years, I've come to realize that thoughtful development is built on three core principles—or what I like to call the three pillars: intentionality, collaboration, and adaptability. These pillars form the foundation of this book, and they're the key to becoming not just a good developer, but a great one.

The first pillar, intentionality, is about being deliberate in everything you do. It's about taking the time to understand the problem you're solving, thinking through your options, and making decisions that align with your goals. I learned the importance of intentionality the hard way on one of my first big projects. We were building a mobile app for a retail company, and the client wanted it done fast. In our rush to deliver, we skipped the planning phase and started coding right away. At first, it felt like we were making great progress, but as the project grew, so did the problems. Features that seemed simple turned out to be complicated because we hadn't thought through the architecture. Bugs kept popping up because we hadn't written enough tests. By the time we launched, the app was barely holding together, and we were all burned out from working late nights to fix last-minute issues. That experience taught me that speed without direction is a recipe for disaster. Thoughtful development means slowing down, asking questions, and making intentional choices that will save you time and effort in the long run.

The second pillar, collaboration, is about recognizing that software development is a team sport. No matter how skilled you are, you can't do it all on your own. I've been on teams where collaboration was an afterthought, and it almost always led to problems. On one project, the designers created a beautiful user interface, but they didn't consult with the developers about whether it was technically feasible. As a result, we ended up with a design that was nearly impossible to implement within the constraints of the project. On another project, the developers didn't involve the testers early enough, so critical bugs weren't caught until late in the process, when they were much harder to fix. These experiences taught me that collaboration isn't just about working together—it's about building a culture of trust, communication, and shared responsibility. Thoughtful development means involving the right people at the right time, listening to their perspectives, and working together to create something better than any of us could achieve on our own.

The third pillar, adaptability, is about embracing change and learning from your mistakes. In a field as fast-moving as software development, the only constant is change. New technologies emerge, requirements shift, and unexpected challenges arise. I've worked on projects where the team resisted change, clinging to outdated tools and processes because "that's the way we've always done it." While it's important to have a solid foundation, I've learned that rigidity can be just as dangerous as chaos. On one project, we started with a monolithic architecture because it was what we were familiar with, but as the application grew, it became clear that a microservices approach would have been a better fit. Making the switch was painful, but it taught me the importance of being open to new ideas and willing to adapt when circumstances change. Thoughtful development means staying curious, learning from your experiences, and being willing to evolve.

These three pillars—intentionality, collaboration, and adaptability—are the foundation of this book. Each chapter is designed to help you build on these principles and apply them to different aspects of software development. But this isn't just a book about theory—it's a practical guide, filled with stories, examples, and actionable advice that you can use in your own work. My goal is to help you not only understand what thoughtful development looks like, but also how to practice it in your day-to-day life as a developer.

As you read through the chapters, I encourage you to approach them with an open mind and a willingness to reflect on your own experiences. Each chapter focuses on a specific aspect of software development, from planning and design to testing and deployment, and offers practical strategies for applying the principles of thoughtful development. For example, in the chapter on design thinking, you'll learn how to involve users in the design process and create solutions that truly meet their needs. In the chapter on debugging, you'll discover how to approach problems systematically and avoid the frustration of trial-and-error fixes. And in the chapter on scaling, you'll explore how to grow your team and your application without losing sight of what made them successful in the first place.

One of the things I've found most helpful when learning new concepts is to set personal goals. As you read each chapter, think about how you can apply what you've learned to your own work. For example, if you're reading the chapter on testing, you might set a goal to write more unit tests or to start using a new testing framework. If you're reading the chapter on time management, you might set a goal to try out a new productivity tool or to block off time for focused work. These goals don't have to be big or ambitious—the important thing is to take small, actionable steps that will help you grow as a developer.

Setting goals isn't just about personal growth—it's also about improving your team. One of the most rewarding parts of my career has been working with teams that share a commitment to thoughtful development. On one project, we set a team goal to improve our code review process. At the time, our reviews were rushed and inconsistent, and it was leading to a lot of avoidable bugs. We decided to create a checklist of best practices for code reviews and to schedule regular review sessions where we could discuss our progress and share feedback. Over time, our reviews became more thorough and constructive, and the quality of our code improved significantly. That experience taught me that setting team goals isn't just about improving processes—it's about building a culture of continuous improvement and shared accountability.

As you work through this book, I encourage you to think about how you can apply the principles of thoughtful development not just to your own work, but to your team as a whole. For example, if you're reading the chapter on collaboration, you might set a team goal to improve communication by holding regular stand-up meetings or by using a shared task management tool. If you're reading the chapter on adaptability, you might set a team goal to experiment with a new technology or to hold a retrospective to reflect on what's working and what's not. These goals can help you create a more thoughtful and effective team, and they can also make your work more enjoyable and fulfilling.

One of the things I've learned about setting goals is that they're most effective when they're specific, measurable, and tied to a larger purpose. On one project, we set a goal to reduce the time it took to onboard new developers. At the time, it was taking weeks for new team members to get up to speed because our documentation was outdated and our processes were inconsistent. We decided to create a detailed onboarding guide and to pair new developers with mentors who could help them navigate the codebase and the team's workflows. Within a few months, we had cut the onboarding time in half, and new developers were feeling more confident and productive. That experience taught me that thoughtful development isn't just about writing better code—it's about creating an environment where everyone can do their best work.

As you read this book, I hope you'll find inspiration and practical advice that you can use to set your own goals and to build a more thoughtful approach to software development. Whether you're just starting out or you've been in the industry for years, there's always room to grow. Thoughtful development isn't a destination—it's a journey, and it's one that we're all on together. By embracing the principles of intentionality, collaboration, and adaptability, we can create software that not only works, but that makes a difference in the lives of the people who use it. And along the way, we can create a more thoughtful, supportive, and fulfilling experience for ourselves and our teams.

CHAPTER TWO

BUILDING THE RIGHT MINDSET

Embracing Continuous Learning

When I first started my career as a developer, I thought success was all about talent. I believed that the best programmers were born with an innate ability to write elegant code, solve complex problems, and pick up new technologies effortlessly. I worked hard, but deep down, I felt like there was a ceiling to what I could achieve. If I struggled to understand a concept or made mistakes, I'd tell myself, "Maybe I'm just not cut out for this." It wasn't until I came across the idea of the growth mindset that my perspective began to shift. I realized that success in software development—or in any field, really—isn't about being naturally gifted. It's about being willing to learn, adapt, and grow.

The growth mindset, a concept popularized by psychologist Carol Dweck, is the belief that abilities and intelligence can be developed through effort, learning, and persistence. It's the opposite of a fixed mindset, which assumes that your skills and talents are static—you either have them or you don't. When I first encountered this idea, it hit me hard. I realized that I had been holding myself back by focusing on what I couldn't do instead of what I could learn. I started to see challenges not as proof of my limitations, but as opportunities to grow. If I didn't understand a new framework or struggled with a tricky bug, it didn't mean I was a bad developer—it just meant I had more to learn.

One of the most transformative moments in my career came when I was working on a project that required me to learn a new programming language. At first, I was overwhelmed. The syntax was unfamiliar, the documentation was dense, and I felt like I was starting from scratch. My initial reaction was frustration—I wanted to give up and stick to the languages I already knew. But then I remembered the growth mindset. Instead of focusing on how hard it was, I started to focus on what I could do to improve. I broke the learning process into small, manageable steps. I wrote simple programs to practice the basics, read blog posts and tutorials, and asked for help from more experienced colleagues. Slowly but surely, I started to get the hang of it. By the end of the project, I wasn't just comfortable with the new language—I was excited to use it in future projects. That experience taught me that learning is a skill in itself, and the more you practice it, the easier it becomes.

In the fast-paced world of software development, embracing continuous learning isn't just a nice-to-have—it's a necessity. Technologies evolve rapidly, and what's cutting-edge today might be obsolete tomorrow. I've seen developers who were once at the top of their game struggle to keep up because they stopped learning. On the other hand, I've worked with developers who thrived because they made learning a regular part of their routine. One of my colleagues, for example, had been in the industry for over 20 years, but he was always the first to try out new tools and frameworks. He'd spend his evenings experimenting with side projects, reading about emerging trends, and sharing what he learned with the team. His curiosity and adaptability were inspiring, and they showed me that staying relevant in this field requires a commitment to lifelong learning.

One of the best ways to stay updated with industry trends is to make learning a habit. For me, this means setting aside time each week to read articles, watch tutorials, or work on side projects. I subscribe to newsletters, follow thought leaders on social media, and attend conferences whenever I can. But staying updated isn't just about consuming information—it's about applying what you learn. On one project, I came across an article about a new testing framework that promised to make writing unit tests faster and more intuitive. I decided to try it out on a small feature I was working on, and it turned out to be a game-changer. Not only did it save me time, but it also made the testing process more enjoyable. I shared my experience with the team, and we ended up adopting the framework for the entire project. That experience taught me that staying updated isn't just about keeping up with trends—it's about finding tools and techniques that can make your work better.

Another important aspect of continuous learning is seeking feedback from your peers. Early in my career, I was hesitant to ask for feedback. I worried that it would make me look inexperienced or that I'd be criticized for my mistakes. But over time, I've come to see feedback as one of the most valuable tools for growth. On one project, I was working on a feature that involved a complex algorithm. I thought I had done a good job, but when I submitted my code for review, one of my colleagues pointed out a flaw in my approach. At first, I felt defensive—I had spent hours on that code, and I didn't want to admit that it wasn't perfect. But as we discussed it, I realized that their feedback wasn't a criticism of me—it was an opportunity to improve. I ended up rewriting the algorithm, and the final result was much better than what I had originally come up with. That experience taught me that feedback isn't something to fear—it's a gift that can help you grow.

Giving and receiving feedback is a skill in itself, and it's one that takes practice. I've learned that the best feedback is specific, constructive, and focused on the work, not the person. On one team, we made it a point to create a culture of open and honest feedback. During code reviews, we'd focus on asking questions and offering suggestions rather than pointing out mistakes. For example, instead of saying, "This code is wrong," we'd say, "Have you considered this approach? It might be more efficient." This approach not only made the feedback process more productive, but it also helped us build trust and respect within the team. I've found that when people feel safe to give and receive feedback, they're more willing to take risks, try new things, and learn from their mistakes.

One of the most powerful lessons I've learned about continuous learning is that it's not just about acquiring new skills—it's about changing the way you think. When you embrace a growth mindset, you start to see challenges as opportunities, feedback as a gift, and mistakes as stepping stones to success. You become more resilient, more curious, and more open to new ideas. And in a field as dynamic as software development, those qualities are invaluable.

Looking back on my career, I can see how much I've grown—not just as a developer, but as a learner. I've gone from fearing challenges to seeking them out, from avoiding feedback to valuing it, and from feeling stuck to feeling empowered. But the journey doesn't end here. Continuous learning is just that—continuous. There will always be new technologies to explore, new skills to master, and new lessons to learn. And that's what makes this field so exciting. Every day is an opportunity to grow, to improve, and to become a more thoughtful, capable, and confident developer.

Discipline and Self-Management

When I first started working as a developer, I thought the key to success was simply putting in more hours. I'd stay late at the office, work through weekends, and pride myself on how much time I was dedicating to my craft. But over time, I realized that working harder wasn't the same as working smarter. I was burning out, making mistakes, and struggling to stay focused. It wasn't until I started paying attention to discipline and self-management that I began to see real progress—not just in my work, but in my overall well-being. Discipline isn't about forcing yourself to work harder; it's about creating the right environment, habits, and mindset to work effectively and sustainably.

One of the first things I learned was the importance of creating a productive workspace. Early in my career, I worked in a chaotic office where distractions were constant. Phones were ringing, conversations were happening all around me, and I found it nearly impossible to focus. I'd try to tune it all out with headphones, but even then, I'd get pulled into impromptu meetings or interrupted by a colleague with a question. It wasn't until I started working remotely that I realized how much my environment affected my productivity. At home, I had the freedom to set up my workspace exactly how I wanted it. I invested in a comfortable chair, a good monitor, and a desk that gave me plenty of room to spread out. I made sure my workspace was well-lit, free of clutter, and separate from the areas where I relaxed. The difference was night and day. With fewer distractions and a space that was dedicated to work, I found it much easier to focus and get into a flow state.

But creating a productive workspace isn't just about the physical setup—it's also about setting boundaries. When I first started working from home, I struggled to separate work from the rest of my life. I'd answer emails late at night, take calls during dinner, and feel like I was always "on." Over time, I realized that this lack of boundaries was taking a toll on my mental health. I started setting clear work hours and sticking to them. I let my team know when I was available and when I wasn't, and I made a point to step away from my desk at the end of the day. These small changes made a big difference. By creating a clear boundary between work and personal time, I was able to recharge and come back to work feeling more focused and energized.

Another game-changer for me was learning how to manage my time effectively. Like many developers, I used to rely on a to-do list to keep track of my tasks. But I often found myself overwhelmed by the sheer number of things I needed to do. I'd jump from one task to another, constantly reacting to whatever seemed most urgent, and by the end of the day, I'd feel like I hadn't accomplished anything meaningful. That's when I discovered time-blocking. Instead of working through a long list of tasks, I started scheduling specific blocks of time for each task on my calendar. For example, I'd set aside an hour in the morning to work on a feature, 30 minutes in the afternoon to review pull requests, and so on. This approach forced me to prioritize my tasks and focus on one thing at a time. It also helped me set realistic expectations for what I could accomplish in a day. I found that by giving each task my full attention during its designated time block, I was able to work more efficiently and with less stress.

Prioritization is another skill that took me a while to master. Early in my career, I had a tendency to focus on the tasks that were easiest or most enjoyable, even if they weren't the most important. I'd spend hours tweaking the design of a feature while neglecting the underlying functionality, or I'd dive into a side project while putting off a critical bug fix. Over time, I learned to ask myself a simple question: "What's the one thing I can do right now that will have the biggest impact?" This question helped me focus on the tasks that truly mattered and let go of the ones that didn't. I also started using a prioritization framework called the Eisenhower Matrix, which categorizes tasks into four quadrants based on their urgency and importance. By focusing on the tasks that were both urgent and important, I was able to make better use of my time and energy.

One of the biggest challenges I've faced as a developer is finding the right balance between speed and quality. In a fast-paced industry like software development, there's often pressure to deliver quickly. Clients want results, managers want progress, and it's easy to fall into the trap of cutting corners to meet deadlines. I've been on projects where we rushed to deliver a feature, only to spend weeks fixing bugs and reworking the code because we didn't take the time to do it right the first time. On the other hand, I've also been on projects where we spent so much time perfecting every detail that we missed our deadlines and frustrated our stakeholders. Finding the right balance isn't easy, but I've learned a few strategies that help.

One of the most important lessons I've learned is that speed and quality aren't mutually exclusive. In fact, taking the time to write clean, well-structured code can often save you time in the long run. On one project, we were building a complex API, and there was pressure to deliver it as quickly as possible. Instead of rushing through the implementation, we took the time to plan the architecture, write tests, and document our decisions. At first, it felt like we were moving slowly, but as the project progressed, we found that the upfront investment paid off. Because the code was well-organized and thoroughly tested, we were able to add new features and fix bugs much more quickly than we would have otherwise. That experience taught me that quality isn't just about writing good code—it's about creating a foundation that allows you to move faster and more confidently in the future.

Another strategy that's helped me balance speed and quality is setting clear expectations with stakeholders. On one project, we were asked to deliver a new feature in just two weeks. We knew it wasn't realistic to build the feature to our usual standards in that timeframe, so we had an honest conversation with the client about what was possible. We agreed to deliver a basic version of the feature by the deadline, with the understanding that we'd refine and improve it in future iterations. This approach allowed us to meet the client's immediate needs without sacrificing the long-term quality of the product. It also taught me the importance of communication and transparency in managing expectations.

Discipline and self-management aren't just about productivity—they're about creating a sustainable way of working. I've learned that taking care of yourself is just as important as taking care of your work. On one project, I was so focused on meeting a tight deadline that I started skipping meals, staying up late, and neglecting my health. By the time the project was finished, I was completely burned out. That experience was a wake-up call. I realized that if I wanted to do my best work, I needed to take care of myself first. Now, I make a point to take regular breaks, eat healthy meals, and get enough sleep. I've also started practicing mindfulness, which helps me stay focused and manage stress. These small changes have made a big difference in my ability to stay disciplined and productive over the long term.

Looking back, I can see how much I've grown in my ability to manage myself and my work. I've gone from feeling overwhelmed and reactive to feeling focused and in control. But self-management is a journey, not a destination. There will always be new challenges to face, new habits to build, and new lessons to learn. By creating a productive workspace, managing your time effectively, and finding the right balance between speed and quality, you can set yourself up for success—not just as a developer, but as a thoughtful, disciplined, and resilient professional..

Motivation and Inspiration

Motivation is a tricky thing. Some days, it feels like you're unstoppable—your ideas flow effortlessly, your code works on the first try, and you're excited about the work you're doing. Other days, it's a struggle just to open your laptop. I've experienced both extremes, and over the years, I've learned that motivation isn't something you can rely on to always be there. It ebbs and flows, and if you don't have strategies to sustain it, you can easily find yourself stuck in a rut. For me, staying motivated has been about setting personal milestones, finding inspiration in the work I do, and learning how to overcome the inevitable challenges of burnout and self-doubt.

One of the most important lessons I've learned about motivation is the power of setting personal milestones. Early in my career, I used to focus entirely on the big picture. I'd think about the final product, the looming deadline, or the long list of features that needed to be built. While it's important to keep the end goal in mind, I found that focusing solely on the big picture often left me feeling overwhelmed. The work ahead seemed endless, and it was hard to see the progress I was making. That's when I started breaking my projects into smaller, more manageable milestones. Instead of thinking about the entire application, I'd focus on completing one feature, fixing one bug, or writing one set of tests. Each milestone became a mini-goal, and every time I completed one, I felt a sense of accomplishment that kept me moving forward.

I remember one project in particular where this approach made all the difference. I was working on a complex data visualization tool for a client, and the scope of the project was massive. At first, I felt paralyzed by the sheer amount of work that needed to be done. But then I broke the project into smaller milestones: first, I'd design the database schema; next, I'd build the API; then, I'd create the front-end components one by one. Each milestone felt achievable, and as I checked them off, I could see the progress I was making. By the time the project was finished, I wasn't just proud of the final product—I was proud of the journey it took to get there. That experience taught me that motivation isn't about tackling everything at once; it's about taking one step at a time and celebrating the progress you make along the way.

Celebrating small wins has become a crucial part of my routine. Early in my career, I used to think that only the big achievements mattered—launching a product, hitting a major deadline, or solving a particularly challenging problem. But I've come to realize that the small wins are just as important. They're the moments that remind you why you love what you do and keep you motivated to keep going. On one project, I spent weeks struggling to fix a performance issue that was causing the application to crash under heavy load. When I finally found the solution, it wasn't a big, dramatic moment—it was a quiet sense of satisfaction as I watched the application run smoothly for the first time. I took a moment to celebrate that win, and it gave me the energy to tackle the next challenge. Those small moments of success are what keep me going, even when the work gets tough.

Another source of motivation for me has been finding inspiration in successful projects. There's something incredibly rewarding about seeing the impact of your work, whether it's a product that makes someone's life easier, a tool that helps a team work more efficiently, or a feature that delights users. I remember one project where we built a mobile app for a nonprofit organization that coordinated disaster relief efforts. The app allowed volunteers to communicate, track resources, and respond to emergencies more effectively. It was a challenging project, with tight deadlines and constantly changing requirements, but seeing the app in action made it all worth it. I'll never forget the moment when one of the volunteers told us how much easier the app had made their work. That experience reminded me why I became a developer in the first place: to solve problems, make a difference, and create something meaningful.

Even when a project isn't as obviously impactful, I try to find inspiration in the work itself. I ask myself questions like: Who will benefit from this? What problem am I solving? How can I make this better? On one project, I was tasked with building an internal tool for a company's HR department. At first, it felt like a mundane assignment—just another form to fill out, another database to query. But as I dug deeper, I realized that the tool had the potential to save the HR team hours of manual work each week. By automating repetitive tasks and streamlining their workflow, I could make their jobs easier and free up their time for more meaningful work. That realization gave me a sense of purpose and motivation, even for a project that might have seemed unremarkable on the surface.

Of course, there are times when motivation is hard to come by, no matter how much you love what you do. Burnout is a real challenge in this industry, and I've experienced it firsthand. On one project, I was juggling multiple deadlines, working long hours, and constantly putting out fires. I started to feel exhausted, both physically and mentally. I'd sit down to work and feel a sense of dread, even for tasks I normally enjoyed. It wasn't until I hit a breaking point that I realized I needed to make a change. I took a step back, talked to my manager about adjusting my workload, and made a conscious effort to take better care of myself. I started setting boundaries, taking regular breaks, and making time for hobbies and activities outside of work. It wasn't an overnight fix, but over time, I started to feel like myself again. That experience taught me that motivation isn't just about pushing through—it's about knowing when to step back, recharge, and take care of yourself.

Another challenge I've faced is imposter syndrome—the feeling that you're not good enough, that you don't belong, or that you're just faking it and will eventually be found out. I've felt this way many times, especially when working with developers who seemed more experienced or talented than me. I'd compare myself to them and feel like I didn't measure up. But over time, I've learned that imposter syndrome is something almost everyone experiences, no matter how skilled or accomplished they are. I've had conversations with senior developers I admire, and they've admitted to feeling the same way. That realization was a turning point for me. It helped me see that self-doubt is normal, and it doesn't mean you're not capable—it just means you're pushing yourself to grow.

One of the best ways I've found to overcome imposter syndrome is to focus on learning and growth. Instead of comparing myself to others, I try to compare myself to where I was yesterday, last month, or last year. I remind myself of the progress I've made and the challenges I've overcome. I also make a point to celebrate my strengths and acknowledge my achievements, no matter how small they might seem. On one project, I was struggling to learn a new framework, and I felt like I was falling behind my teammates. But then I reminded myself that just a few months earlier, I hadn't even heard of the framework, and now I was building features with it. That shift in perspective helped me see that I wasn't failing—I was learning.

Motivation and inspiration aren't always easy to find, but they're essential for building the right mindset as a developer. By setting personal milestones, finding meaning in your work, and learning how to navigate challenges like burnout and imposter syndrome, you can stay motivated even when the road gets tough. And when you do, you'll not only become a better developer—you'll also find more joy and fulfillment in the work you do.

CHAPTER THREE

Strategic Planning Before You Code

Requirement Gathering

When I first started working as a developer, I thought the most important part of my job was writing code. I believed that as long as I could deliver a working product, everything else would fall into place. But it didn't take long for me to realize that the success of a project doesn't start with the code—it starts with understanding the problem you're solving. And that understanding comes from effective requirement gathering. If you don't take the time to gather clear, detailed requirements upfront, you're setting yourself up for confusion, frustration, and a lot of wasted effort. I've learned this lesson the hard way, and over the years, I've developed a deep appreciation for the importance of communication, documentation, and building a shared understanding with stakeholders.

One of the biggest challenges in requirement gathering is effective communication with stakeholders. Stakeholders come in all shapes and sizes—clients, managers, end users, and even other developers—and each one has their own perspective, priorities, and expectations. Early in my career, I made the mistake of assuming that stakeholders always knew exactly what they wanted. I'd sit down with a client, listen to their ideas, and then dive straight into development without asking too many questions. Inevitably, this approach led to problems. On one project, I was building a scheduling tool for a small business. The client told me they wanted a "simple calendar app," so that's what I built. But when I delivered the first version, they were disappointed. It turned out that what they really needed was a system for managing recurring appointments, sending reminders, and tracking customer preferences—none of which I had included. The problem wasn't that I had written bad code; it was that I hadn't taken the time to truly understand their needs.

That experience taught me the importance of asking the right questions. Instead of taking stakeholder requests at face value, I've learned to dig deeper. I ask questions like, "What problem are you trying to solve?" "Who will be using this feature?" and "What does success look like for this project?" These questions help me get to the root of what the stakeholders really need, rather than just what they think they want. On one project, I was working with a nonprofit organization that wanted a tool for tracking donations. At first, they described it as a simple database for storing donor information. But as we talked more, I realized that their real goal was to improve donor engagement. By asking questions and listening carefully, I was able to suggest features like automated thank-you emails, donation history reports, and integration with their marketing tools. The final product was much more valuable to them than the basic database they had originally envisioned.

Another key to effective communication is managing expectations. Stakeholders often have high hopes for what a project can achieve, but they may not fully understand the technical constraints or trade-offs involved. I've been on projects where stakeholders asked for features that sounded simple but were actually incredibly complex to implement. On one project, a client wanted a real-time chat feature for their website. They assumed it would be as easy as adding a plugin, but in reality, it required significant backend work, server resources, and ongoing maintenance. Instead of just saying "yes" and struggling to deliver, I've learned to have honest conversations about what's realistic. I explain the effort involved, discuss alternative solutions, and work with the stakeholders to prioritize the features that will have the biggest impact. These conversations aren't always easy, but they're essential for building trust and ensuring that everyone is on the same page.

Once you've gathered the initial requirements, the next step is documenting them clearly. I used to think documentation was a tedious chore, but I've come to see it as one of the most important parts of the development process. Without clear documentation, it's easy for misunderstandings to arise. Stakeholders might assume you're building one thing while you're actually building something else, and by the time you realize the disconnect, it's often too late. On one project, I was working with a team to build an e-commerce platform. We had a series of meetings with the client to discuss their requirements, but we didn't document the details. As a result, different team members had different interpretations of what the client wanted. One developer started building a custom checkout flow, while another was integrating a third-party payment gateway. When we finally compared notes, we realized we were heading in completely different directions. That experience taught me that even the best conversations are meaningless if you don't capture the outcomes in writing.

When documenting project requirements, I try to be as specific and detailed as possible. Instead of vague statements like "The app should be user-friendly," I write concrete descriptions like "The app should include a three-step onboarding process with tooltips to guide new users." I also include wireframes, flowcharts, and examples whenever possible, as visual aids can help clarify complex ideas. On one project, I was working with a client who wanted a dashboard for tracking sales metrics. Instead of just describing the features in text, I created a mockup that showed how the dashboard would look and function. The client was able to provide feedback early in the process, which saved us from making costly changes later on. Clear documentation not only helps align expectations but also serves as a reference point throughout the project. If questions or disagreements arise, you can always go back to the original specs to clarify what was agreed upon.

But requirement gathering isn't just about communication and documentation—it's also about building a shared understanding among everyone involved. I've been on projects where different stakeholders had conflicting priorities, and it was up to the development team to navigate the tension. On one project, the marketing team wanted a flashy, feature-rich website, while the operations team wanted something simple and easy to maintain. If we had tried to please everyone, we would have ended up with a bloated, unfocused product. Instead, we brought all the stakeholders together for a workshop where we discussed their goals, priorities, and constraints. By facilitating an open dialogue, we were able to find common ground and agree on a clear direction for the project. That experience taught me that building a shared understanding isn't just about gathering information—it's about fostering collaboration and alignment.

One of the most effective ways I've found to build a shared understanding is through user stories. User stories are short, simple descriptions of a feature from the perspective of the end user. For example, instead of saying "The app should have a login page," you might write, "As a user, I want to log in with my email and password so that I can access my account." User stories help keep the focus on the user's needs and provide a common language that everyone can understand. On one project, we used user stories to map out the entire user journey, from signing up to completing a purchase. This approach helped us identify gaps in the requirements and ensured that everyone—developers, designers, and stakeholders—was aligned on what we were building and why.

Looking back, I can see how much my approach to requirement gathering has evolved. I've gone from rushing through the process to seeing it as the foundation of every successful project. By communicating effectively with stakeholders, documenting clear project specs, and building a shared understanding, I've been able to avoid many of the pitfalls that can derail a project. But more importantly, I've learned that requirement gathering isn't just about collecting information—it's about building relationships, fostering collaboration, and setting the stage for thoughtful, intentional development. When you take the time to get it right, you're not just setting yourself up for success—you're creating a better experience for everyone involved.

Problem Definition and Scope

One of the most important lessons I've learned as a developer is that you can't solve a problem you don't fully understand. Early in my career, I often jumped straight into coding as soon as I received a project brief. I'd start building features, writing tests, and piecing everything together, only to realize halfway through that I didn't actually know what problem I was solving. I'd end up with a product that was functional but didn't meet the client's needs—or worse, a product that solved the wrong problem entirely. Over time, I've come to see problem definition as the foundation of any successful project. If you don't take the time to define the core problem and establish clear boundaries, you're setting yourself up for confusion, wasted effort, and frustration.

I remember one project in particular that taught me the importance of defining the core problem. A client approached us with a request to build a mobile app for their business. They wanted an app that would "improve customer engagement," but beyond that, their requirements were vague. Excited to get started, we dove into development without asking too many questions. We built a sleek app with a loyalty program, push notifications, and a social media integration. But when we presented it to the client, they were underwhelmed. It turned out that their real problem wasn't customer engagement—it was customer retention. They were losing customers because their competitors offered better deals, and no amount of push notifications was going to fix that. If we had taken the time to dig deeper and define the core problem, we could have built something that actually addressed their needs, like a price-matching feature or a personalized discount system.

That experience taught me to always start by asking, "What problem are we trying to solve?" It's a deceptively simple question, but it can uncover a lot of hidden assumptions. On another project, I was working with a team to build a task management tool for a startup. The initial request was to create a "better version of Trello." But as we talked to the stakeholders, we realized that their real problem wasn't that Trello was bad—it was that their team struggled with prioritization and accountability. By focusing on the core problem, we were able to design a tool that included features like priority tagging, deadline reminders, and team progress tracking. The final product wasn't just a copy of Trello—it was a solution tailored to their specific needs.

Defining the core problem also helps you avoid one of the biggest pitfalls in software development: feature creep. Feature creep happens when a project's scope expands beyond its original goals, often because stakeholders keep adding new features or changing their minds about what they want. I've been on projects where feature creep turned a simple, three-month project into a year-long ordeal. On one project, we were building an e-commerce platform for a small business. The original plan was straightforward: a product catalog, a shopping cart, and a checkout system. But as we progressed, the client kept requesting additional features—a blog, a customer review system, a loyalty program, and so on. Each new feature seemed small on its own, but together, they added up to a massive increase in complexity. By the time we finished, the project was months behind schedule, and the client was frustrated with the delays.

To avoid feature creep, I've learned to set clear boundaries at the start of a project. This means defining not just what the project will include, but also what it won't include. On one project, we were building a scheduling tool for a healthcare provider. During the planning phase, we worked with the client to create a detailed scope document that outlined the core features: appointment booking, calendar integration, and automated reminders. We also explicitly listed the features that were out of scope, like patient record management and billing. This document became our north star throughout the project. Whenever the client requested a new feature, we referred back to the scope document and asked, "Does this align with the core problem we're solving?" If the answer was no, we added the feature to a backlog for future consideration, rather than trying to squeeze it into the current project. This approach helped us stay focused and deliver the project on time.

Another strategy I've found helpful for managing scope is using simple checklists. Checklists might seem basic, but they're incredibly effective for maintaining clarity and alignment. On one project, we were building a dashboard for tracking sales metrics. During the planning phase, we created a checklist of the key features and requirements, like "Display monthly sales data," "Allow users to filter by region," and "Export data to CSV." This checklist became a shared reference point for the entire team. It helped us stay focused on the core features, and it made it easy to track our progress. Whenever a stakeholder asked about the status of the project, we could point to the checklist and show exactly what was done and what was still in progress. It also helped us avoid scope creep, because any new feature requests had to be added to the checklist and approved by the stakeholders before we started working on them.

Checklists are also a great tool for ensuring that everyone has a shared understanding of the project. On one project, we were building a mobile app for a fitness startup. During the planning phase, we created a checklist of user stories, like "As a user, I want to log my workouts so that I can track my progress" and "As a user, I want to set fitness goals so that I can stay motivated." These user stories helped us stay focused on the user's needs, and they provided a common language that everyone—developers, designers, and stakeholders—could understand. Whenever there was a question or disagreement about a feature, we referred back to the user stories to clarify what we were building and why.

Defining the core problem, managing scope, and using checklists might not sound as exciting as writing code, but they're some of the most important skills a developer can have. They're the foundation of strategic planning, and they can save you a lot of time, effort, and frustration in the long run. I've learned this lesson the hard way, through projects that went off the rails because we didn't take the time to plan properly. But I've also seen the benefits of getting it right. On one project, we were building a customer support tool for a SaaS company. By defining the core problem (improving response times), setting clear boundaries (focusing on chat and email support, not phone support), and using a checklist to track our progress, we were able to deliver a product that exceeded the client's expectations—on time and within budget.

Looking back, I can see how much my approach to problem definition and scope has evolved. I've gone from rushing into development to taking the time to ask questions, set boundaries, and create a clear plan. It's not always easy—stakeholders can be impatient, and it's tempting to skip the planning phase and start coding. But I've learned that the time you spend upfront defining the problem and managing the scope is an investment that pays off in the end. It leads to better products, happier clients, and a more enjoyable development process. And for me, that's what thoughtful development is all about.

Mapping Out the Development Plan

When I first started working on software projects, I thought planning was just a formality. I believed the real work began when I started writing code, and everything else was just paperwork. But after a few chaotic projects where deadlines slipped, budgets ballooned, and everyone was scrambling to figure out what went wrong, I realized how critical it is to map out a clear development plan before writing a single line of code. A good plan isn't just a document—it's a guide that keeps the entire team aligned, helps you anticipate challenges, and ensures that the project stays on track. Over the years, I've learned that tools like Gantt charts, roadmaps, and milestone tracking aren't just for project managers—they're essential for developers too.

One of the first projects where I truly understood the value of a development plan was a mobile app for a fitness startup. The client wanted a sleek, feature-rich app that allowed users to track workouts, set goals, and connect with friends. It was an ambitious project with a tight deadline, and at first, I was overwhelmed by the sheer amount of work that needed to be done. But instead of diving straight into development, we took a step back and created a roadmap. We broke the project into phases—design, backend development, frontend development, testing, and deployment—and mapped out each phase on a Gantt chart. The chart showed not only the timeline for each phase but also how they overlapped. For example, while the designers were working on the user interface, the backend team could start building the API. This overlap allowed us to work more efficiently and avoid bottlenecks.

The Gantt chart also helped us identify dependencies. For instance, the frontend team couldn't start integrating the API until the backend team had finished building it. By mapping out these dependencies, we were able to plan our work in a way that minimized delays. On one occasion, we realized that a critical API endpoint wouldn't be ready in time for the frontend team to start their work. Instead of waiting, we created a mock API that allowed the frontend team to proceed with development while the backend team finished their work. This kind of foresight wouldn't have been possible without a clear roadmap.

Estimating timelines and costs is another crucial part of mapping out a development plan. Early in my career, I struggled with this. I'd give optimistic estimates based on how long I thought a task should take, rather than how long it would realistically take. Inevitably, things would take longer than expected, and I'd end up scrambling to meet deadlines. On one project, I estimated that building a custom reporting feature would take two weeks. But I didn't account for the time needed to gather requirements, test the feature, and fix bugs. In the end, it took over a month, and the delay threw off the entire project timeline.

After that experience, I started taking a more methodical approach to estimating timelines. Instead of relying on gut feelings, I began breaking tasks into smaller, more manageable pieces and estimating the time for each piece individually. For example, instead of estimating how long it would take to build an entire feature, I'd estimate the time needed to design the database schema, write the API endpoints, and create the frontend components. I also started factoring in time for testing, debugging, and unexpected challenges. On one project, we used a technique called "three-point estimation," where we calculated the best-case, worst-case, and most likely time for each task. This approach gave us a more realistic picture of the timeline and helped us set expectations with the client.

Cost estimation is closely tied to timeline estimation. On one project, we were building a web app for a small business, and the client had a limited budget. By breaking the project into phases and estimating the cost of each phase, we were able to prioritize the most important features and deliver a functional product within their budget. For example, instead of building a custom analytics dashboard, we integrated a third-party tool that met their needs at a fraction of the cost. This kind of trade-off wouldn't have been possible without a clear understanding of the project's scope, timeline, and budget.

Tracking milestones is another key part of a successful development plan. Milestones are like checkpoints that help you measure progress and ensure that the project is on track. On one project, we set milestones for completing the design phase, finishing the backend API, and launching the beta version of the app. Each milestone had a specific deadline, and we used a project management tool to track our progress. Whenever we reached a milestone, we took a moment to review our work, celebrate our progress, and adjust our plan if needed. For example, after completing the design phase, we realized that some of the features were more complex than we had anticipated. By identifying this early, we were able to adjust our timeline and allocate more resources to those features.

Tracking workload is just as important as tracking milestones. On one project, I was part of a small team building a scheduling tool for a healthcare provider. At first, we divided the work evenly among the team members, but we quickly realized that some tasks were much more time-consuming than others. One developer was overwhelmed with backend work, while another had finished their frontend tasks and was waiting for more work. To address this, we started tracking each team member's workload and redistributing tasks as needed. This not only helped us work more efficiently but also prevented burnout.

One of the most valuable lessons I've learned about tracking milestones and workload is the importance of flexibility. No matter how well you plan, things will go wrong. Features will take longer than expected, bugs will pop up, and stakeholders will change their minds. On one project, we were building a real-time chat feature for a customer support tool. Halfway through development, the client decided they wanted to add video chat functionality. This was a major change that required significant backend work, and it threatened to derail the entire project. Instead of panicking, we revisited our roadmap, adjusted our milestones, and reallocated resources to accommodate the change. It wasn't easy, but because we had a clear plan in place, we were able to adapt without losing sight of the project's overall goals.

Looking back, I can see how much my approach to planning has evolved. I've gone from seeing planning as a formality to recognizing it as an essential part of the development process. By creating Gantt charts and roadmaps, estimating timelines and costs, and tracking milestones and workload, I've been able to deliver projects more efficiently and with less stress. But more importantly, I've learned that a good plan isn't just about meeting deadlines—it's about creating a shared vision, building trust with stakeholders, and setting the stage for thoughtful, intentional development. When you take the time to map out a clear development plan, you're not just setting yourself up for success—you're creating a better experience for everyone involved.

CHAPTER FOUR

Design Thinking for Developers

Empathize and Define

I'll never forget the first time I worked on a project where we completely missed the mark because we didn't take the time to understand the users. It was a scheduling app for a small business, and the client had given us a list of features they wanted: a calendar, notifications, and a way to assign tasks to employees. It all seemed straightforward, so we jumped right into development. We built the app exactly as requested, with a sleek interface and all the features the client had asked for. But when we delivered the final product, the client wasn't happy.

The problem wasn't the code or the design—it was that the app didn't actually solve the users' problems. The employees found it confusing to use, and the business owner said it didn't save them any time. We had focused so much on building the features that we forgot to ask the most important question: *What do the users really need?*

That experience taught me the importance of empathy in development. As developers, it's easy to get caught up in the technical details—choosing the right frameworks, writing clean code, optimizing performance. But at the end of the day, the success of a product depends on how well it meets the needs of its users. And the only way to do that is to take the time to understand those needs.

Empathy starts with listening. When I worked on a project for a nonprofit organization, we spent the first few weeks interviewing the people who would be using the product. These were volunteers who were often juggling multiple responsibilities and didn't have a lot of time to learn new tools. We asked them about their daily routines, the challenges they faced, and what they wished they had to make their work easier.

One volunteer told us about how they struggled to keep track of their assignments because they were spread across multiple emails and spreadsheets. Another mentioned that they often missed important updates because they didn't have time to check their email during the day. These conversations gave us valuable insights into the pain points we needed to address.

But understanding user needs isn't just about listening—it's also about observing. Sometimes, users can't articulate what they need because they don't know what's possible. I've found that watching people interact with existing tools or workflows can reveal problems they might not even be aware of. For example, when we observed the volunteers at the nonprofit, we noticed that many of them were using their phones to check their assignments, even though the existing system wasn't optimized for mobile. This insight helped us prioritize mobile-friendly design in the new product.

Once you've gathered insights about your users, the next step is to organize that information in a way that helps you make better decisions. One of the most effective tools I've used for this is creating user personas. A persona is a fictional character that represents a specific type of user. It's based on real data and insights, but it's presented in a way that makes it easy to understand and remember.

For example, when we were working on the nonprofit project, we created a persona called "Busy Brenda." Brenda was a volunteer who worked full-time and only had a few hours a week to dedicate to the nonprofit. She relied on her phone to stay connected and needed a tool that was simple, fast, and easy to use. By keeping Brenda in mind throughout the development process, we were able to make design decisions that prioritized her needs.

Personas are especially helpful when you're working with a team. They give everyone a shared understanding of who the users are and what they care about. I've been on projects where team members had different ideas about who the product was for, which led to conflicting priorities and wasted effort. By creating personas and referring back to them regularly, you can keep everyone aligned and focused on the users.

Another tool I've found useful is creating use cases. A use case is a specific scenario that describes how a user interacts with a product to achieve a goal. For example, one of the use cases for the nonprofit project was: "Brenda wants to check her assignments on her phone during her lunch break." This use case helped us think through the details of the user experience, such as how quickly the app needed to load, how easy it was to navigate, and how the information was presented on a small screen.

Use cases are a great way to bridge the gap between user needs and technical requirements. They help you think about the product from the user's perspective while also considering the practicalities of implementation. I've found that writing use cases early in the development process can save a lot of time and effort later on because they help you anticipate potential issues and make better decisions upfront.

Once you have a clear understanding of your users and their needs, the next step is to define the design criteria for your product. Design criteria are the principles and goals that guide your decisions throughout the development process. They're like a compass that keeps you on track and ensures that every feature, every line of code, and every design element serves a purpose.

I've learned that setting the right design criteria is all about balance. On one hand, you want to be ambitious and create something that exceeds your users' expectations. On the other hand, you need to be realistic about what's achievable within the constraints of your project.

For example, when we were working on the nonprofit project, one of our design criteria was "Make it easy for volunteers to find their assignments in less than 30 seconds." This was a clear, measurable goal that helped us prioritize simplicity and speed in the user interface. At the same time, we had to balance this with other criteria, such as "Ensure the system is secure and compliant with privacy regulations."

I've found that it's helpful to involve stakeholders in the process of setting design criteria. This ensures that everyone is aligned on the goals of the project and helps prevent misunderstandings later on. For example, when we presented our design criteria to the nonprofit's leadership team, they emphasized the importance of accessibility for older volunteers who might not be tech-savvy. This feedback led us to prioritize features like larger text sizes and a simple, intuitive interface.

One of the biggest challenges in setting design criteria is avoiding the temptation to include too much. It's easy to get carried away and try to solve every problem or address every user need. But I've learned that the best products are the ones that do a few things really well, rather than trying to do everything.

For example, when we were working on a project for a fitness app, the client initially wanted to include features like meal planning, workout tracking, and social networking. But after talking to users and setting design criteria, we realized that the core value of the app was helping people stay consistent with their workouts. By focusing on this core problem, we were able to create a product that was simple, effective, and loved by users.

At the end of the day, design thinking is about putting yourself in the shoes of your users and making decisions that prioritize their needs. It's about listening, observing, and empathizing. It's about creating tools like personas and use cases to keep your team aligned and focused. And it's about setting clear, realistic design criteria that guide your decisions and help you deliver a product that truly makes a difference.

The next time you start a project, take the time to empathize with your users and define the problem you're solving. Don't rush into development without understanding who you're building for and what they need. Because when you take the time to listen, observe, and plan, you're not just building a product—you're creating something that has the power to improve people's lives. And that's what thoughtful development is all about.

Ideate Potential Solutions

I remember a project early in my career where we were tasked with building a mobile app for a local food delivery service. The client wanted something that could compete with the big players in the market, but they didn't have a clear vision of what the app should look like or how it should function. They just knew they wanted it to be "better" than their competitors. It was a daunting challenge, and as a team, we felt stuck. We had a vague idea of the problem we were solving—making food delivery faster and more convenient—but we didn't know where to start when it came to designing the solution.

That's when I learned the value of brainstorming. At the time, I thought brainstorming was just a fancy word for sitting in a room and throwing out random ideas. But when done right, it's so much more than that. It's a structured process that helps you generate creative solutions, explore different perspectives, and uncover ideas you might not have considered otherwise.

For the food delivery app, we started with a simple technique: mind mapping. We wrote the core problem—"improving the food delivery experience"—in the center of a whiteboard and started branching out from there. One branch focused on the user experience: How could we make the app easier to use? Another branch explored logistics: How could we reduce delivery times? A third branch looked at customer engagement: How could we encourage repeat orders?

As we added more branches and sub-branches, the whiteboard filled up with ideas. Some were practical, like offering real-time tracking for deliveries. Others were more outlandish, like using drones to deliver food. But the beauty of mind mapping is that it encourages you to think freely and explore all possibilities without judgment. At this stage, there are no bad ideas—just opportunities to think outside the box.

Once we had a mind map full of ideas, the next step was to evaluate their feasibility and impact. This is where things get tricky because you have to balance creativity with practicality. It's easy to get excited about a flashy idea, but if it's too expensive, time-consuming, or technically challenging to implement, it might not be worth pursuing.

For the food delivery app, we used a simple framework to evaluate each idea:

- **Feasibility:** How easy is it to implement this idea with the resources we have?
- **Impact:** How much value will this idea provide to the users and the business?

For example, real-time tracking scored high on both feasibility and impact. It was relatively straightforward to implement using GPS technology, and it addressed a major pain point for users who wanted to know exactly when their food would arrive. On the other hand, drone delivery scored low on feasibility—it would have required significant investment in hardware and regulatory approvals—and its impact was questionable since most users were happy with traditional delivery methods.

By evaluating each idea in this way, we were able to narrow down our options and focus on the ones that offered the best balance of feasibility and impact. This process not only helped us prioritize our efforts but also gave us a clear direction for the next phase of the project.

One of the most valuable lessons I've learned is that you don't have to commit to a solution right away. In fact, it's often better to test your ideas through rapid prototyping before you invest too much time and effort into development. Prototyping allows you to explore different solutions, gather feedback, and refine your ideas based on real-world insights.

For the food delivery app, we started with low-fidelity prototypes—simple sketches and wireframes that showed the basic layout and functionality of the app. We used these prototypes to conduct user testing with a small group of customers. We asked them to complete tasks like placing an order or tracking a delivery and observed how they interacted with the interface.

One of the most surprising insights we gained from this testing was that users wanted more control over their delivery experience. For example, some users wanted the option to schedule deliveries in advance, while others wanted to leave specific instructions for the delivery driver. These were features we hadn't considered during the brainstorming phase, but they became key components of the final product.

After refining the low-fidelity prototypes based on user feedback, we moved on to high-fidelity prototypes—interactive mockups that looked and felt more like the final app. These prototypes allowed us to test more advanced features, like real-time tracking and push notifications, and gather additional feedback from users.

One of the biggest challenges we faced during the prototyping phase was managing expectations. Some stakeholders expected the prototypes to be fully functional, while others didn't understand why we were spending time on prototypes instead of jumping straight into development. To address this, we made a point of explaining the purpose of prototyping: to test ideas, identify potential issues, and ensure that we were building the right solution before investing in full-scale development.

Prototyping isn't just about testing functionality—it's also about exploring different design options and finding the one that works best for your users. For example, during the prototyping phase of the food delivery app, we experimented with different layouts for the order confirmation screen. One version displayed the delivery time in large, bold text at the top of the screen, while another version included a map showing the driver's location. Through user testing, we discovered that users preferred the map because it gave them a sense of control and reassurance.

Another important aspect of prototyping is iteration. It's rare to get everything right on the first try, so it's important to be open to feedback and willing to make changes. For the food delivery app, we went through several iterations of the user interface before we landed on a design that met the needs of both the users and the business. Each iteration brought us closer to the final product and helped us avoid costly mistakes later on.

One of the most rewarding moments of the project came when we launched the app and started receiving feedback from real users. Many of the features we had brainstormed, prototyped, and refined—like real-time tracking and the ability to schedule deliveries—were praised by users for making their lives easier. It was a reminder of why design thinking is so important: by taking the time to understand user needs, explore potential solutions, and test your ideas, you can create products that truly make a difference.

Looking back, I realize that the success of the food delivery app wasn't just about the technology or the design—it was about the process we followed. By using brainstorming techniques like mind mapping, evaluating the feasibility and impact of our ideas, and testing our solutions through rapid prototyping, we were able to create a product that met the needs of both the users and the business.

The next time you're faced with a challenging problem, don't be afraid to think outside the box and explore different solutions. Use tools like mind maps to generate ideas, evaluate their feasibility and impact to prioritize your efforts, and test your ideas through rapid prototyping to ensure that you're on the right track. Because at the end of the day, design thinking isn't just about solving problems—it's about creating solutions that truly matter.

Refine and Validate

I'll never forget a project I worked on for a small startup that wanted to build a platform for connecting freelancers with clients. The idea was exciting, and the team was passionate about creating something innovative. We had gone through the initial phases of brainstorming and prototyping, and we felt confident about the direction we were heading. But as we moved closer to development, cracks started to appear. The design looked great on paper, but when we tested it with a few users, we realized it wasn't as intuitive as we thought. Users struggled to navigate the interface, and some of the features we thought were essential didn't resonate with them at all.

That experience taught me the importance of refining and validating designs before jumping into full-scale development. It's easy to fall in love with your initial ideas, but the truth is, no design is perfect on the first try. The best products are the result of an iterative process—one where you continuously review, refine, and validate your work based on real feedback.

One of the most valuable lessons I've learned is that design is never "done." It's a living, evolving process that requires constant iteration. On the freelancer platform project, we started holding regular design reviews with the team. These weren't just casual meetings where we looked at the latest mockups and nodded in agreement. They were structured sessions where we critically evaluated every aspect of the design, from the user flows to the visual elements.

During one of these reviews, a developer pointed out that the onboarding process was too long and complicated. We had designed a multi-step tutorial to guide new users through the platform, but it turned out to be overwhelming. Users were dropping off before they even completed the signup process. This feedback was hard to hear because we had spent a lot of time perfecting the tutorial, but it was exactly what we needed to improve the design.

We went back to the drawing board and simplified the onboarding process. Instead of a lengthy tutorial, we created a short, interactive walkthrough that highlighted the key features of the platform. We tested the new design with a small group of users, and the results were night and day. Users were able to get started quickly, and engagement rates improved significantly.

This iterative approach to design review taught me the importance of collaboration. As developers, designers, and stakeholders, we all bring different perspectives to the table. By working together and challenging each other's assumptions, we can create better solutions. I've found that the best design reviews are the ones where everyone feels comfortable sharing their honest opinions, even if it means pointing out flaws or suggesting changes.

Another key lesson I've learned is the value of collecting feedback early and often. It's tempting to wait until you have a polished design before showing it to users, but the earlier you gather feedback, the easier it is to make changes. On the freelancer platform project, we started testing our designs with users as soon as we had rough wireframes. These early tests weren't about getting everything right—they were about identifying major issues and validating our assumptions.

For example, one of our early wireframes included a feature that allowed clients to post detailed project descriptions. We thought this would be a key selling point, but when we tested it with users, we discovered that freelancers found it overwhelming. They didn't want to read long descriptions—they wanted a quick summary of the project and the client's expectations. This insight led us to redesign the feature, focusing on brevity and clarity.

Collecting feedback early also helps you avoid costly mistakes. I've seen projects where teams spent months perfecting a design, only to discover during user testing that it didn't meet the needs of their audience. By testing early and iterating based on feedback, you can catch these issues before they become major problems.

Of course, collecting feedback isn't just about listening to users—it's also about interpreting their feedback and deciding how to act on it. Not every piece of feedback will be useful, and sometimes users will have conflicting opinions. I've found that the key is to look for patterns and focus on the underlying problems. For example, if multiple users are struggling with the same feature, it's a sign that something needs to change.

One of the most challenging aspects of refining and validating designs is knowing when to stop iterating. It's easy to get caught in a cycle of endless revisions, especially if you're a perfectionist. But at some point, you need to move forward and start building. On the freelancer platform project, we set clear goals for each iteration and defined what "good enough" looked like. This helped us stay focused and avoid getting stuck in the refinement phase.

Once we were confident in the design, the next step was handing it off to the development team. This might sound like a straightforward process, but it's actually one of the most critical—and often overlooked—phases of the project. A smooth handoff can make the difference between a successful implementation and a frustrating experience for everyone involved.

I've been on projects where the design handoff was rushed or poorly organized, and it always led to problems. Developers would start building without fully understanding the design, and the final product would end up looking and functioning differently than intended. To avoid this, I've learned to treat the handoff as a collaborative process, not just a one-time transfer of files.

For the freelancer platform project, we held a series of handoff meetings where the designers walked the developers through the final mockups, explaining the rationale behind each decision and answering any questions. We also provided detailed documentation, including style guides, component libraries, and interaction specifications. This ensured that everyone was on the same page and had the information they needed to bring the design to life.

One of the most effective tools we used during the handoff was a design system. This was a collection of reusable components, such as buttons, forms, and navigation elements, that were consistent across the platform. By using a design system, we were able to streamline the development process and ensure that the final product matched the original vision.

Another important aspect of the handoff was maintaining open communication between the designers and developers throughout the development process. Even with the best documentation, questions and challenges are bound to come up. By fostering a culture of collaboration and mutual respect, we were able to address these issues quickly and keep the project on track.

Looking back, I realize that the success of the freelancer platform wasn't just about the final product—it was about the process we followed to refine and validate the design. By embracing an iterative approach, collecting feedback early, and ensuring a smooth handoff to development, we were able to create a platform that met the needs of both freelancers and clients.

The lessons I learned from that project have stayed with me ever since. Whether I'm working on a small feature or a large-scale application, I always remind myself that design is a journey, not a destination. It's about listening, learning, and adapting. It's about collaborating with your team and your users to create something that truly makes a difference.

So the next time you're working on a project, don't be afraid to revisit your designs, gather feedback, and make changes. Treat the handoff to development as an opportunity to collaborate and ensure that your vision is realized. Because at the end of the day, thoughtful design isn't just about what you create—it's about how you create it. And when you approach the process with care and intention, you're not just building a product—you're building something that people will love.

Architecture and Technical Blueprint

Choosing the Right Architecture

I remember a project I worked on a few years ago for a fast-growing e-commerce startup. They wanted to build a platform that could handle thousands of daily transactions, support a growing catalog of products, and integrate with third-party services like payment gateways and shipping providers. The team was excited, and we were eager to get started. But before we wrote a single line of code, we had to answer a critical question: *What kind of architecture should we use?*

At first, the answer seemed obvious. A monolithic architecture—where the entire application is built as a single, unified codebase—was the simplest and fastest option. It would allow us to get the platform up and running quickly, and since the team was small, it seemed manageable. But as we dug deeper into the requirements, we started to question whether a monolith was the right choice.

The startup had ambitious plans for growth. They wanted to expand into new markets, add features like personalized recommendations and real-time inventory tracking, and eventually support millions of users. We realized that while a monolithic architecture might work in the short term, it could become a bottleneck as the platform scaled. For example, if one part of the application—like the product catalog—needed to handle a sudden surge in traffic, the entire system could be affected.

That's when we started exploring other options, like microservices. Unlike a monolith, a microservices architecture breaks the application into smaller, independent services that communicate with each other through APIs. Each service is responsible for a specific function, like managing user accounts or processing payments, and can be developed, deployed, and scaled independently.

The idea of microservices was appealing because it aligned with the startup's long-term goals. If the platform needed to handle more traffic, we could scale individual services without affecting the rest of the system. If we wanted to add new features, we could build them as separate services without disrupting the existing codebase. And since each service could use its own technology stack, we had the flexibility to choose the best tools for each job.

But microservices also came with trade-offs. They added complexity to the system, requiring us to manage multiple codebases, deploy services independently, and handle communication between them. For a small team with limited resources, this was a significant challenge. We had to ask ourselves: *Is the added complexity worth it?*

To answer that question, we looked at the startup's immediate needs. While scalability was important, the platform didn't need to handle millions of users on day one. The priority was to launch quickly and start generating revenue. With that in mind, we decided to start with a monolithic architecture and transition to microservices as the platform grew. This approach allowed us to balance simplicity and scalability, giving the startup a solid foundation to build on.

Another option we considered was serverless architecture, where the application is built using cloud-based functions that automatically scale based on demand. Serverless was an attractive choice because it eliminated the need to manage servers and infrastructure, allowing us to focus on writing code. It also offered built-in scalability, which was perfect for handling unpredictable traffic patterns.

However, serverless wasn't a perfect fit for this project. While it worked well for certain use cases, like event-driven applications or lightweight APIs, it wasn't ideal for a complex e-commerce platform with multiple interconnected features. We also had concerns about vendor lock-in, since serverless functions are often tied to specific cloud providers. Ultimately, we decided that a monolithic architecture was the best starting point, with the option to incorporate serverless components for specific tasks, like image processing or sending notifications.

One of the biggest lessons I've learned from this project—and others like it—is that there's no one-size-fits-all solution when it comes to architecture. Each pattern has its strengths and weaknesses, and the right choice depends on your specific needs, goals, and constraints.

For example, monolithic architectures are great for small teams and projects with straightforward requirements. They're easy to develop, test, and deploy, and they don't require the overhead of managing multiple services. But as the application grows, a monolith can become harder to maintain and scale.

Microservices, on the other hand, are ideal for large, complex systems that need to scale independently. They allow teams to work on different parts of the application simultaneously, using the tools and technologies that best suit their needs. But they also require careful planning and coordination to avoid issues like service dependencies, data consistency, and communication overhead.

Serverless architectures are perfect for applications with variable workloads or event-driven use cases. They offer automatic scaling, reduced infrastructure costs, and faster time to market. But they're not always the best choice for applications with complex workflows or high-performance requirements, and they can introduce challenges like cold starts and vendor lock-in.

When choosing an architecture, it's important to think about scalability from day one. Even if your application doesn't need to handle millions of users right away, you should plan for growth. This doesn't mean you need to over-engineer your system, but you should choose an architecture that can evolve as your needs change.

For example, on the e-commerce project, we designed the monolithic architecture with scalability in mind. We used a modular approach, organizing the codebase into separate components for each feature, like the product catalog, shopping cart, and payment processing. This made it easier to transition to microservices later on, since each component could be extracted into its own service.

We also used a scalable database solution, opting for a cloud-based platform that could handle increasing traffic and data volume. This allowed us to focus on building the application without worrying about database performance.

Another important consideration is the trade-offs involved in each architectural pattern. No matter which approach you choose, there will always be compromises. The key is to understand these trade-offs and make informed decisions based on your priorities.

For example, if speed to market is your top priority, a monolithic architecture might be the best choice, even if it's not the most scalable option. If you're building a system that needs to handle unpredictable traffic spikes, serverless might be worth the trade-offs in complexity and vendor lock-in. And if you're working on a large, distributed system with multiple teams, microservices might be the way to go, even if it requires more coordination and infrastructure management.

At the end of the day, choosing the right architecture is about finding the balance that works for your project. It's about understanding your goals, evaluating your options, and making decisions that set you up for success—not just today, but in the future.

The e-commerce project taught me that architecture isn't just about technology—it's about strategy. It's about thinking ahead, anticipating challenges, and building a system that can adapt to change. Whether you're working on a small startup or a large enterprise, the principles are the same: start with a clear understanding of your needs, weigh the trade-offs, and choose an architecture that aligns with your vision.

Because at the end of the day, the best architecture isn't the one with the most features or the latest buzzwords—it's the one that helps you achieve your goals and deliver value to your users. And that's what thoughtful development is all about.

Technology Stack Decisions

I once worked on a project for a mid-sized company that wanted to build a customer relationship management (CRM) tool tailored to their specific needs. They had tried off-the-shelf solutions, but none of them quite fit their workflows. The project was ambitious, and the team was excited to dive in. But before we could start building, we had to make some critical decisions about the technology stack. What language should we use? Which frameworks and tools would best support the project? These questions might seem straightforward, but they're anything but simple. The choices you make at this stage can have long-term consequences, affecting everything from performance and security to how quickly your team can deliver features.

The first step in making these decisions was to evaluate the options available to us. For the CRM project, we had to consider the core requirements: the system needed to handle a large amount of data, support real-time updates, and integrate with third-party services like email and payment gateways. We also wanted a stack that would allow us to build a responsive, user-friendly interface.

Initially, there was a lot of debate about which programming language to use. Some team members advocated for Python because of its simplicity and the wide range of libraries available for data processing and integration. Others pushed for JavaScript, arguing that it would allow us to use the same language for both the front-end and back-end, which could streamline development. A few even suggested Java, citing its performance and scalability.

To make an informed decision, we created a list of criteria to evaluate each option. We looked at factors like performance, ease of use, community support, and compatibility with the tools we wanted to use. For example, Python was a strong contender because of its readability and the availability of frameworks like Django, which could help us build the back-end quickly. However, we ultimately chose JavaScript because it allowed us to use Node.js for the back-end and React for the front-end, creating a unified stack that made it easier for developers to switch between tasks.

One of the biggest lessons I've learned from projects like this is that there's no perfect language or framework. Every option has its strengths and weaknesses, and the right choice depends on your specific needs. For the CRM project, JavaScript wasn't the fastest or most secure language, but it offered the flexibility and developer productivity we needed to meet our goals.

Once we had chosen the language, the next step was to select the frameworks and tools that would form the foundation of the system. This was another area where we had to weigh trade-offs. For example, we considered using a full-stack framework like Meteor, which would have allowed us to build the entire application with minimal setup. However, we decided against it because we wanted more control over the architecture and the ability to swap out components as needed.

Instead, we opted for a modular approach, using React for the front-end, Node.js for the back-end, and PostgreSQL for the database. React was a natural choice because of its component-based architecture, which made it easy to build and maintain a complex user interface. Node.js was a good fit for the back-end because of its non-blocking I/O model, which allowed us to handle real-time updates efficiently. And PostgreSQL offered the performance and reliability we needed for managing large amounts of data.

One of the challenges we faced during this process was balancing performance and security. For example, we wanted the system to be fast and responsive, but we also needed to ensure that sensitive customer data was protected. This led to some tough decisions, like whether to use a relational database or a NoSQL database. NoSQL databases like MongoDB are often faster for certain types of queries, but they don't always offer the same level of data integrity and security as relational databases. In the end, we chose PostgreSQL because it provided the best balance of performance and security for our use case.

Another area where performance and security came into play was in choosing third-party tools and libraries. For example, we needed a library for handling authentication, and we considered several options, including building our own solution. While a custom solution would have given us more control, it would also have been time-consuming and error-prone. Instead, we chose a well-established library with a strong track record of security and community support. This decision saved us time and reduced the risk of vulnerabilities in the system.

One of the most important factors in choosing a technology stack is the expertise of your team. Even the best tools and frameworks are useless if your team doesn't know how to use them effectively. On the CRM project, we had a team of developers who were already familiar with JavaScript and React, which made it easier to get up to speed. If we had chosen a language like Ruby or a framework like Angular, we would have faced a steep learning curve, which could have delayed the project.

That's not to say you should always stick with what you know. Sometimes, it's worth investing in new tools or technologies if they offer significant advantages. For example, on another project, we decided to use TypeScript instead of plain JavaScript because it provided better type safety and improved developer productivity. While it took some time for the team to learn TypeScript, the benefits outweighed the initial effort.

The key is to strike a balance between leveraging your team's existing skills and exploring new technologies that can help you achieve your goals. If you're introducing a new tool or framework, it's important to provide training and support to help your team succeed. On the CRM project, we held regular workshops and code reviews to ensure that everyone was comfortable with the stack and following best practices.

Looking back, I realize that choosing the right technology stack is as much about people as it is about technology. It's about understanding your team's strengths and weaknesses, aligning your choices with your project's goals, and being willing to adapt as new challenges arise.

The CRM project was a success, not because we chose the "best" tools, but because we chose the tools that were right for us. By evaluating our options carefully, considering performance and security, and leveraging our team's expertise, we were able to build a system that met the client's needs and delivered real value.

The next time you're faced with a technology stack decision, remember that it's not just about the tools—it's about how those tools fit into your overall strategy. Take the time to evaluate your options, involve your team in the decision-making process, and don't be afraid to make trade-offs. Because at the end of the day, the best stack isn't the one with the most features or the latest buzzwords—it's the one that helps you build something meaningful.

Creating a Robust Technical Blueprint

I once worked on a project for a logistics company that wanted to modernize its operations. They had an outdated system that relied heavily on manual processes, and they needed a new platform to manage everything from inventory tracking to delivery scheduling. The scope was massive, and it was clear from the start that we couldn't afford to dive into development without a solid plan. That's when I truly understood the importance of creating a robust technical blueprint. It's not just about having a high-level idea of what you're building—it's about mapping out every layer, every connection, and every potential challenge before you write a single line of code.

The first step in creating the blueprint was to visualize the application's structure. For the logistics platform, we used a layered approach to break the system into manageable pieces. At the top was the presentation layer, which included the user interfaces for both desktop and mobile. Beneath that was the application layer, where the business logic lived—things like calculating delivery routes or managing inventory levels. At the bottom was the data layer, which handled storage and retrieval from the database.

This layered approach wasn't just about organizing the system—it was about creating a clear separation of concerns. Each layer had a specific role, and changes in one layer wouldn't ripple through the others. For example, if we decided to redesign the user interface, we could do so without touching the business logic or the database. This made the system more flexible and easier to maintain.

To make sure everyone on the team understood the architecture, we created detailed diagrams for each layer. These weren't just static images—they were living documents that evolved as the project progressed. For the presentation layer, we mapped out the different screens and how users would navigate between them. For the application layer, we outlined the key services and how they interacted with each other. And for the data layer, we created an entity-relationship diagram to show how the data was structured and how it would be accessed.

One of the biggest challenges we faced was mapping out the data flow and integration points. The logistics platform needed to pull data from multiple sources, including third-party APIs for tracking shipments and a legacy system that stored historical data. It also needed to push data to external systems, like the company's accounting software.

To tackle this, we started by identifying all the integration points and documenting how data would flow between them. For example, when a new delivery was scheduled, the system needed to send the details to the accounting software to generate an invoice. At the same time, it needed to update the inventory system to reflect the items being shipped.

We used flow diagrams to visualize these processes, showing how data moved through the system and where potential bottlenecks or failures could occur. This helped us identify areas that needed special attention, like ensuring data consistency between the legacy system and the new platform. It also helped us plan for error handling—what would happen if an API call failed, or if the legacy system was temporarily unavailable?

One of the most valuable tools we used during this phase was an architecture checklist. This wasn't a formal document—it was more like a set of guiding questions that we revisited throughout the project. For example:

- Does the architecture support the system's scalability requirements?
- Have we accounted for security at every layer?
- Are the integration points clearly defined and documented?
- Do we have a plan for monitoring and troubleshooting?

The checklist helped us stay focused and ensure that we weren't overlooking any critical details. For example, during one of our reviews, we realized that we hadn't fully considered how the system would handle large spikes in traffic. The logistics company often experienced surges during peak seasons, like the holidays, and we needed to make sure the platform could scale to meet demand. This led us to revisit the application layer and implement a queuing system to handle high volumes of requests without overwhelming the database.

Another item on the checklist was security. The logistics platform dealt with sensitive data, like customer addresses and payment information, so we needed to ensure that it was protected at every step. This meant encrypting data in transit and at rest, implementing role-based access control, and conducting regular security audits. By including these considerations in the blueprint, we were able to address them early in the development process, rather than scrambling to fix them later.

One of the most rewarding moments of the project came when we presented the technical blueprint to the stakeholders. They weren't technical experts, but the diagrams and flowcharts helped them understand how the system would work and how it would address their pain points. This not only gave them confidence in the project but also helped us get their buy-in for some of the more complex features, like real-time tracking and automated notifications.

Looking back, I realize that the success of the logistics platform wasn't just about the technology—it was about the planning. By taking the time to create a robust technical blueprint, we were able to anticipate challenges, align the team around a shared vision, and build a system that met the company's needs.

The lessons I learned from that project have stayed with me ever since. Whether I'm working on a small app or a large enterprise system, I always start with a blueprint. It's not just a document—it's a roadmap that guides every decision and keeps the project on track.

If there's one piece of advice I'd give to anyone starting a new project, it's this: don't skip the blueprint. Take the time to map out your architecture, visualize your data flow, and create a checklist to keep yourself accountable. It might feel like extra work upfront, but it will save you countless hours—and headaches—down the road. Because at the end of the day, a well-thought-out blueprint isn't just a plan for building a system—it's a foundation for success.

CHAPTER SIX

Writing Clean and Efficient Code

Coding Standards and Best Practices

I still remember one of my first big projects as a developer. It was a web application for a small business, and I was eager to prove myself. I worked long hours, pouring all my energy into writing code as quickly as possible. By the time the project was ready for testing, I felt proud of what I had accomplished. But when my team started reviewing the code, the feedback was brutal. Variable names were inconsistent, functions were bloated and hard to follow, and there were strange bugs popping up in places I didn't expect. One of my colleagues even joked that my code looked like it had been written by three different people.

At first, I was defensive. The application worked, didn't it? But as I sat down with my team to go through the code, I began to see their point. The lack of consistency made it hard for anyone else to understand or maintain the code. Debugging was a nightmare because I hadn't followed any clear structure. That experience taught me a valuable lesson: writing clean and efficient code isn't just about making something work—it's about making it understandable, maintainable, and scalable for the long term.

One of the first things I learned was the importance of consistent naming conventions and formatting. It might seem like a small detail, but it makes a huge difference when you're working on a team or revisiting your own code months later. On that project, I had used a mix of naming styles—some variables were written in camelCase, others in snake_case, and a few were just single letters. It was confusing, even for me.

After that experience, I started following established naming conventions. For example, I began using camelCase for variables and functions, and PascalCase for class names. I also made sure that variable names were descriptive enough to convey their purpose. Instead of something vague like **x** or **temp**, I'd use names like **userEmail** or **orderTotal**. It might take a little more time upfront, but it saves countless hours when you or someone else needs to understand the code later.

Formatting was another area where I had to improve. In my early days, I didn't pay much attention to things like indentation, spacing, or line length. But as I started working on larger projects, I realized how much easier it was to read and navigate code that followed a consistent format. Now, I always use tools like linters and code formatters to enforce standards automatically. It's a simple step, but it ensures that everyone on the team is writing code in the same style, which makes collaboration much smoother.

Another lesson I learned was the importance of avoiding anti-patterns and bad smells in code. Early in my career, I didn't even know what these terms meant. But as I gained more experience, I started to recognize the signs of poorly written code—things like overly complex functions, duplicated logic, and unnecessary dependencies.

One of the worst habits I had was writing functions that tried to do too much. I remember one function in particular that was over 200 lines long. It handled everything from validating user input to querying the database and rendering the response. At the time, I thought I was being efficient by cramming everything into one place. But when a bug appeared, it was almost impossible to figure out where the problem was.

After that, I started following the single responsibility principle, which states that each function or class should have one clear purpose. By breaking the code into smaller, more focused pieces, I made it easier to test, debug, and reuse. For example, instead of one massive function, I'd create separate functions for input validation, database queries, and response rendering. Each function was only a few lines long, and it was immediately clear what it was supposed to do.

I also learned to watch out for duplicated code. On that same project, I had copied and pasted the same block of code into multiple places because I thought it was faster than refactoring. But when the requirements changed, I had to update each instance of the code manually, and I inevitably missed a few. Now, whenever I see duplicated logic, I refactor it into a reusable function or class. It might take a little more effort upfront, but it saves time and reduces the risk of errors in the long run.

One of the most effective ways to improve code quality is through peer reviews and code walkthroughs. Early in my career, I dreaded code reviews. It felt like my work was being scrutinized, and I was afraid of being judged. But over time, I came to see them as an opportunity to learn and grow.

On one project, I was working on a feature that involved complex calculations for generating reports. I thought I had done a good job, but during the code review, a colleague pointed out that my implementation was unnecessarily complicated. They suggested a simpler approach that not only reduced the amount of code but also made it easier to understand. That experience taught me that code reviews aren't about criticism—they're about collaboration.

Now, I actively seek out feedback from my peers. Before submitting code for review, I try to walk through it myself, asking questions like: *Is this code easy to understand? Could it be simplified? Are there any edge cases I haven't considered?* By the time I submit it, I've already caught many of the issues that might have come up during the review.

I've also learned the value of participating in code walkthroughs, where the author of the code explains their thought process to the team. These sessions are a great way to share knowledge, identify potential problems, and ensure that everyone understands how the code works. They're especially helpful for onboarding new team members, as they provide context that might not be immediately obvious from reading the code alone.

Looking back, I realize that writing clean and efficient code isn't just a technical skill—it's a mindset. It's about taking pride in your work and recognizing that your code will be read, used, and maintained by others. It's about striving for clarity, simplicity, and consistency, even when you're under pressure to deliver quickly.

The lessons I've learned—about naming conventions, avoiding anti-patterns, and embracing peer reviews—have made me a better developer. They've also made me a better teammate, because clean code isn't just easier to work with—it's a sign of respect for the people who will come after you.

So the next time you sit down to write code, take a moment to think about the person who will read it next. Will they understand what you were trying to do? Will they be able to build on your work without tearing it apart? If the answer is yes, then you're not just writing code—you're crafting something that will stand the test of time. And that's what clean, efficient code is all about.

Modularity and Reusability

I'll never forget the first time I had to revisit a project I'd written months earlier. It was a simple web application for managing tasks, and at the time, I thought I had done a great job. The app worked, the client was happy, and I moved on to other projects. But when the client came back asking for a few new features, I found myself staring at my own code, completely lost. The problem wasn't that the code was broken—it was that it was repetitive, tangled, and anything but modular. Adding a new feature meant making the same changes in multiple places, and every tweak seemed to break something else. What should have been a quick update turned into a frustrating, time-consuming ordeal.

That experience taught me the importance of modularity and reusability in code. Writing code that works is one thing, but writing code that can grow and adapt without falling apart is a whole different challenge. It starts with identifying repetitive code blocks—those little snippets that seem to pop up over and over again in slightly different forms.

On that task management app, for example, I had written nearly identical code for displaying tasks in different parts of the application. There was one block of code for the main task list, another for the "completed tasks" section, and yet another for the search results. Each block handled things like formatting the task name, showing the due date, and adding buttons for editing or deleting the task. At the time, it seemed easier to just copy and paste the code and make a few tweaks. But when the client asked for a new feature—color-coding tasks based on priority—I had to update each of those blocks individually. It was tedious, error-prone, and completely avoidable.

After that project, I made a habit of looking for patterns in my code. If I found myself writing the same logic more than once, I'd stop and ask: *Can this be turned into a reusable function or component?* For example, instead of duplicating the task display logic, I could have created a single function that took a task object as input and returned the formatted HTML. That way, any changes to the display logic would only need to be made in one place.

Designing reusable components and functions isn't just about saving time—it's about creating a foundation that makes your code easier to understand, test, and maintain. On a later project, I worked on a dashboard for a financial services company. The dashboard had multiple charts, tables, and widgets, many of which shared similar functionality, like filtering data or exporting reports. Instead of building each feature from scratch, we created a library of reusable components.

For example, we built a generic table component that could handle sorting, filtering, and pagination. Each table in the dashboard used this component, passing in the specific data and configuration it needed. This approach not only saved us time during development but also made the codebase more consistent. If we needed to update the table functionality—like adding a new export option—we could do it in one place, and the change would automatically apply to every table in the application.

Creating reusable components requires a bit of foresight. You have to think about how the component might be used in different contexts and design it to be flexible enough to handle those scenarios. For the table component, we made sure it could accept custom column definitions, so each table could display different types of data. We also added hooks for custom actions, like opening a modal or triggering an API call when a row was clicked. By anticipating these needs upfront, we avoided the need to rewrite or heavily modify the component later.

Of course, you don't always have to build everything from scratch. One of the most valuable lessons I've learned is to leverage existing libraries and packages whenever possible. Early in my career, I had a tendency to reinvent the wheel. If I needed a date picker, I'd write my own. If I needed to validate a form, I'd create my own validation logic. It wasn't until I started working on larger projects with tight deadlines that I realized how much time and effort I was wasting.

On one project, we needed to implement a complex data visualization feature. My initial instinct was to build it from the ground up, but a colleague suggested using a library like D3.js. At first, I was hesitant—I worried that the library might not do exactly what we needed, or that it would add unnecessary complexity. But after spending some time with the documentation, I realized that D3.js could handle most of the heavy lifting, and we could customize it to fit our requirements. By using the library, we were able to deliver the feature in a fraction of the time it would have taken to build it ourselves.

The key to using libraries and packages effectively is to choose them carefully. Not every library is a good fit for your project, and relying too heavily on third-party code can introduce risks, like security vulnerabilities or compatibility issues. Before adopting a library, I always ask a few questions: *Is it actively maintained? Does it have good documentation? Does it solve the problem better than I could on my own?* If the answer to these questions is yes, then it's usually worth using.

One of the best examples of leveraging libraries came on a project where we needed to implement authentication. Instead of building our own system, we used a library that handled everything from password hashing to token generation. This not only saved us time but also ensured that we were following best practices for security—something that's easy to get wrong when you're rolling your own solution.

Looking back, I realize that modularity and reusability aren't just about writing better code—they're about working smarter. By identifying repetitive patterns, designing reusable components, and leveraging existing tools, you can create systems that are easier to build, maintain, and scale.

The task management app that once felt like a tangled mess could have been so much simpler if I had approached it with these principles in mind. And the projects I've worked on since then have been far more enjoyable—and successful—because I've taken the time to think about how to make my code modular and reusable from the start.

So the next time you're writing code, take a step back and ask yourself: *Am I solving this problem in the most efficient way? Can this logic be reused elsewhere? Is there a library that could save me time?* By asking these questions, you'll not only write better code—you'll become a better developer. And that's a skill that will serve you well, no matter what kind of project you're working on.

Performance Optimization

I'll never forget the time I worked on a project for a retail company that wanted to build an online store capable of handling thousands of users during peak sales events. The initial version of the platform worked fine during development and testing, but when we launched it during a promotional event, everything fell apart. Pages were taking forever to load, some users couldn't even complete their purchases, and the client was understandably frustrated. It was a wake-up call for me and the team: we had focused so much on building features that we had neglected to think about performance. That experience taught me that writing clean and efficient code isn't just about making it readable—it's also about making it fast and scalable.

The first step in addressing the performance issues was figuring out where the bottlenecks were. At the time, I didn't have much experience with profiling tools, so I relied on guesswork and trial-and-error. I'd tweak a piece of code, test it, and hope for the best. It was a slow and frustrating process. Eventually, a more experienced developer on the team introduced me to profiling tools, and it was like a lightbulb went off.

We used a tool to analyze the application's performance, and it quickly became clear where the problems were. For example, we discovered that a database query used to load product details was taking far longer than expected. Every time a user visited a product page, the application was fetching the same data from the database instead of caching it. By adding a caching layer, we were able to reduce the load time for product pages from several seconds to just a fraction of a second.

Profiling tools also helped us identify inefficient loops in the code. In one case, we had a function that iterated over a large dataset multiple times to calculate discounts for a shopping cart. By refactoring the function to perform all the calculations in a single pass, we were able to cut the processing time in half. These kinds of optimizations might seem small, but they add up quickly, especially when you're dealing with high traffic.

Another lesson I learned from that project was the importance of memory and resource management. One of the biggest issues we faced was that the application was consuming far more memory than it should have been. This was causing the server to slow down and, in some cases, crash under heavy load.

When we dug into the problem, we found that the application was holding onto objects in memory long after they were no longer needed. For example, we had a function that loaded a list of products into memory, but it wasn't releasing the memory after the function was done. This might not have been a big deal for a small dataset, but when the list contained thousands of products, it became a serious problem.

To fix this, we started paying closer attention to how memory was being allocated and released. We used tools to monitor memory usage and identify areas where we could improve. For example, we replaced some of the in-memory data structures with more efficient alternatives, like streams that processed data on the fly instead of loading everything into memory at once. We also made sure to explicitly release resources, like database connections and file handles, as soon as we were done with them.

One of the most valuable techniques we used was lazy loading, which involves loading data only when it's needed. For example, instead of loading all the product images for a page at once, we loaded only the images that were visible to the user and fetched the rest as they scrolled. This not only reduced memory usage but also improved the perceived performance of the application, since users didn't have to wait for everything to load before they could start interacting with the page.

Of course, optimizing performance isn't just about fixing problems—it's also about writing efficient code from the start. One of the biggest mistakes I made early in my career was assuming that "working code" was good enough. I'd write a function that got the job done, without thinking about whether it was the most efficient way to solve the problem.

On one project, I wrote a function to search for items in a list. The function worked fine during testing, but when the list grew to thousands of items, it became painfully slow. The problem was that I was using a linear search, which checked each item in the list one by one. By switching to a more efficient algorithm, like binary search, I was able to improve the performance dramatically.

That experience taught me to think about the efficiency of my code, even for seemingly small tasks. For example, I now pay close attention to the complexity of algorithms and try to use the most efficient data structures for the job. If I'm working with a large dataset, I'll use a hash map instead of a list for lookups, or a priority queue instead of a simple array for sorting. These kinds of optimizations might not always be necessary, but they can make a big difference when performance is critical.

Another technique I've found useful is minimizing the number of network requests. On one project, we had a feature that required fetching data from multiple APIs. Initially, we made separate requests for each piece of data, which worked fine during development. But when we tested the feature with real-world data, the delays started to add up. By combining the requests into a single batch and processing the data on the server, we were able to reduce the load time significantly.

Looking back, I realize that performance optimization is as much about mindset as it is about tools and techniques. It's about being proactive—identifying potential bottlenecks before they become problems, managing resources carefully, and writing efficient code from the start. It's also about being willing to revisit and refine your work, even if it means rewriting code that already "works."

The retail platform that once struggled under heavy load eventually became a success, thanks to the lessons we learned about performance optimization. And those lessons have stayed with me ever since. Whether I'm working on a small app or a large-scale system, I always take the time to think about how my code will perform—not just today, but as the system grows and evolves.

Because at the end of the day, writing clean and efficient code isn't just about making something that works—it's about making something that works well, no matter how big the challenge. And that's what performance optimization is all about.

TEST EARLY, TEST OFTEN

Testing Fundamentals

I learned the importance of testing the hard way. Early in my career, I worked on a project for a small startup that was building a scheduling app. The team was small, the deadlines were tight, and we were all eager to deliver something impressive. Testing, at the time, felt like a luxury we couldn't afford. We were so focused on getting features out the door that we didn't stop to think about how those features would hold up under real-world conditions.

The app launched on schedule, and for the first few days, everything seemed fine. But then the bug reports started rolling in. Users were complaining about appointments disappearing, notifications being sent at the wrong times, and the app crashing when they tried to sync their calendars. It was chaos. We spent weeks scrambling to fix the issues, often breaking other parts of the app in the process. It was a painful experience, but it taught me a lesson I've carried with me ever since: testing isn't optional. It's an essential part of building software that works.

One of the first things I learned about testing is that it's not a one-size-fits-all process. There are different types of tests, each with its own purpose and scope. Unit tests, for example, focus on individual pieces of code, like functions or methods. They're like the building blocks of a testing strategy, ensuring that each part of the system works as expected in isolation.

I remember working on a feature for a financial app that calculated loan payments based on interest rates, loan terms, and other factors. It was a complex formula, and I wanted to make sure it was rock-solid. Writing unit tests for the calculation function allowed me to test it with a variety of inputs, including edge cases like zero interest rates or extremely long loan terms. By the time I integrated the function into the app, I was confident that it worked correctly because I had already tested it in isolation.

But unit tests are only the beginning. Once you've verified that individual components work, you need to test how they interact with each other. That's where integration tests come in. On the scheduling app, for example, we had a feature that allowed users to sync their appointments with external calendar services like Google Calendar. The syncing process involved multiple components: the user interface, the back-end API, and the third-party calendar service.

Initially, we only tested these components separately, and everything seemed fine. But when we tried syncing appointments end-to-end, we ran into all sorts of issues. Some appointments weren't syncing at all, while others were being duplicated. It turned out that the components weren't communicating with each other as expected. If we had written integration tests to simulate the syncing process, we could have caught these issues much earlier.

End-to-end (E2E) tests take things a step further by testing the entire system from the user's perspective. They're like a final safety net, ensuring that everything works together as it should. On one project, I worked on an e-commerce platform where users could browse products, add them to their cart, and complete a purchase. Writing E2E tests for the checkout process allowed us to simulate a user's journey through the app, from selecting a product to receiving a confirmation email. These tests gave us confidence that the system would work as expected in the real world, even as we made changes to individual components.

Of course, writing tests is only part of the equation. You also need a testing environment that mirrors the production environment as closely as possible. On the scheduling app, one of the reasons we ran into so many issues was that our testing environment didn't include the third-party calendar services we were integrating with. We were testing in isolation, which meant we weren't catching issues that only appeared when the app interacted with external systems.

On later projects, I made it a priority to set up a robust testing environment. For example, on the e-commerce platform, we created a staging environment that included a copy of the production database and mocked versions of third-party services like payment gateways. This allowed us to test the system under realistic conditions without risking real user data. We also used tools like Docker to ensure that the testing environment was consistent across different machines, so developers could reproduce issues locally before deploying fixes.

One of the biggest challenges with testing is convincing stakeholders that it's worth the time and effort. In fast-paced environments, there's often pressure to skip testing in favor of delivering features more quickly. But skipping testing is a false economy. Bugs that go undetected during development are much more expensive to fix later, especially if they make it into production.

I've found that the best way to demonstrate the value of testing is to focus on the return on investment (ROI). Automated testing, in particular, can save a tremendous amount of time and effort in the long run. On the financial app, for example, we had a suite of automated tests that ran every time we made a change to the codebase. These tests caught several issues before they made it into production, saving us from having to roll back changes or issue emergency fixes.

Automated testing also makes it easier to refactor code. On one project, we needed to rewrite a large part of the codebase to improve performance. Without tests, this would have been a risky and time-consuming process, as we would have had to manually verify that everything still worked. But because we had a comprehensive suite of automated tests, we were able to make the changes with confidence, knowing that the tests would catch any regressions.

That's not to say that automated testing is a silver bullet. Writing and maintaining tests takes time, and not every test is worth automating. For example, tests that cover rarely used features or edge cases might not provide enough value to justify the effort. The key is to focus on the areas that matter most, like critical business logic or high-traffic parts of the system.

One of the most rewarding moments of my career came on a project where we had invested heavily in automated testing. The client wanted to add a major new feature to the app, and they were worried about how it would affect the existing functionality. But because we had a robust testing strategy in place, we were able to implement the feature quickly and with minimal risk. When we deployed the update, everything worked seamlessly, and the client was thrilled.

Looking back, I realize that testing isn't just about finding bugs—it's about building confidence. It's about knowing that your code will work as expected, even as the system grows and evolves. It's about creating a safety net that allows you to move quickly without breaking things.

The lessons I've learned about testing have transformed the way I approach software development. Whether I'm writing unit tests for a small function, setting up a staging environment, or advocating for automated testing, I always keep one principle in mind: test early, test often. Because the sooner you catch an issue, the easier it is to fix—and the more time you'll have to focus on building something great.

Testing might not be the most glamorous part of software development, but it's one of the most important. It's the difference between a system that works and one that fails under pressure. And in the end, it's what separates good developers from great ones.

Effective Testing Strategies

I'll never forget the first time I worked on a project where testing was treated as an afterthought. It was a small internal tool for a company, something that was supposed to be quick and simple. The team was under pressure to deliver fast, so we skipped writing tests and focused entirely on getting the features out the door. At first, everything seemed fine. The tool worked during our initial demos, and the client was happy. But as soon as it went live, the problems started. Bugs appeared in places we hadn't anticipated, and fixing one issue often broke something else. Every time we deployed a patch, we held our breath, hoping we hadn't introduced new problems. It was a stressful, chaotic experience, and it could have been avoided if we had taken testing seriously from the start.

That project taught me a hard but valuable lesson: testing isn't optional. It's not something you tack on at the end of development—it's an integral part of the process. Over the years, I've learned that effective testing isn't just about writing a few unit tests and calling it a day. It's about adopting strategies that ensure your code is reliable, maintainable, and ready for the real world. And two of the most powerful strategies I've encountered are Test-Driven Development (TDD) and Behavior-Driven Development (BDD).

The first time I tried TDD, I'll admit, it felt counterintuitive. The idea of writing tests before writing the actual code seemed backward. I was used to diving straight into coding, solving problems as they came up, and then writing tests (if I had time). But on one project—a complex API for a financial services company—I decided to give TDD a try. The API had to handle sensitive data, perform complex calculations, and integrate with multiple third-party services. It was the kind of project where even small mistakes could have big consequences, so I knew we needed a robust testing strategy.

With TDD, the process started by writing a failing test for each feature we wanted to implement. For example, one of the first features was calculating interest on a loan. Before writing any code, I wrote a test that defined the expected behavior: given a loan amount, an interest rate, and a time period, the function should return the correct interest. Of course, the test failed initially because the function didn't exist yet. But that failure was the point—it gave me a clear goal to work toward.

Once the test was in place, I wrote just enough code to make it pass. At first, the implementation was simple, even crude. I hardcoded the result for a specific set of inputs, just to see the test turn green. Then, I refactored the code to handle a wider range of inputs, running the test after each change to ensure I hadn't broken anything. By the time the function was complete, I had not only a working implementation but also a set of tests that would catch any future regressions.

What I loved about TDD was how it forced me to think about the requirements before writing any code. Instead of guessing what the function should do, I had to define its behavior in concrete terms. This made the code more focused and less prone to edge cases I might have overlooked otherwise. It also gave me confidence that the code was doing what it was supposed to do, even as the project grew more complex.

But TDD isn't the only testing strategy that's had a big impact on my work. On another project—a web application for a healthcare startup—I had the chance to use Behavior-Driven Development (BDD). While TDD focuses on testing individual units of code, BDD takes a higher-level approach, focusing on the behavior of the system as a whole. It's about bridging the gap between developers, testers, and stakeholders by using a shared language to describe how the system should behave.

For the healthcare app, we used a BDD framework called Cucumber. The process started with writing "feature files" in plain English, describing the desired behavior of the application. For example, one feature was allowing patients to book appointments online. The feature file included scenarios like:

- Given a patient is logged in, when they select a doctor and a time slot, then the appointment should be booked successfully.
- Given a time slot is already booked, when a patient tries to select it, then they should see an error message.

These scenarios were written in collaboration with the stakeholders, who didn't have technical backgrounds but understood the business requirements. Once the feature files were written, we implemented the underlying code to make the scenarios pass. This process felt a lot like TDD, but with a stronger focus on the user's perspective.

What I appreciated about BDD was how it encouraged collaboration. Instead of developers working in isolation, we were constantly communicating with stakeholders to ensure we were building the right thing. It also made the tests more meaningful. Instead of abstract unit tests, we had scenarios that directly reflected the user's needs. This made it easier to prioritize features and catch issues that might have slipped through the cracks.

Of course, testing strategies like TDD and BDD are only part of the equation. Another critical aspect of effective testing is ensuring good code coverage and integrating tests into your development workflow. On one project, I worked with a team that used continuous integration (CI) to run tests automatically every time we pushed code to the repository. At first, I didn't see the point. Why run the same tests over and over again? But as the project grew, I realized how valuable CI was.

One day, I made what seemed like a small change to a utility function. I didn't think it would affect anything else, so I didn't bother running the tests locally. But when I pushed the code, the CI pipeline flagged a failing test. It turned out that the function was used in a completely different part of the application, and my change had introduced a subtle bug. Without CI, I might not have caught the issue until much later, when it would have been harder to fix.

Code coverage tools were another game-changer for me. On one project, we used a tool to measure how much of the codebase was covered by tests. At first, the results were embarrassing—less than 50% of the code was tested. But instead of getting discouraged, we used the coverage report as a roadmap. We identified the most critical parts of the application and focused on writing tests for those areas first. Over time, we increased the coverage to over 90%, which gave us much more confidence in the stability of the system.

That said, I've also learned that code coverage isn't everything. It's possible to have 100% coverage and still miss important bugs if the tests aren't meaningful. For example, I've seen tests that simply check whether a function runs without throwing an error, without verifying that it produces the correct result. Effective testing isn't just about quantity—it's about quality. The goal is to write tests that catch real-world issues and ensure the system behaves as expected.

Looking back, I realize that testing has transformed the way I approach development. Strategies like TDD and BDD have made my code more reliable and easier to maintain, while tools like CI and code coverage have helped me catch issues early and avoid costly mistakes. But perhaps the most important lesson I've learned is that testing isn't just a technical practice—it's a mindset. It's about taking responsibility for the quality of your work and recognizing that every bug you catch today is one less headache for your team (and your users) tomorrow.

The healthcare app, the financial API, the retail platform—all of these projects taught me that effective testing isn't just about writing tests. It's about building a culture of quality, where testing is an integral part of the development process, not an afterthought. And when you embrace that mindset, you're not just writing code—you're building systems that people can trust. And that, in the end, is what great software is all about.

Troubleshooting and Debugging

Debugging is one of those skills that every developer learns, but few truly master. Early in my career, I thought debugging was just about finding and fixing errors as quickly as possible. I'd dive into the code, make a few guesses, and hope for the best. Sometimes I got lucky, but more often than not, I'd spend hours chasing the wrong problem or introducing new bugs in the process. It wasn't until I worked on a particularly challenging project that I realized debugging isn't just about fixing problems—it's about understanding them. And the key to effective debugging is having a systematic approach.

I remember one project in particular that taught me this lesson. It was a real-time chat application for a client who wanted to integrate it into their customer support system. Everything was going smoothly until we started testing the app under load. Messages were being delayed, some weren't being delivered at all, and the server logs were filled with cryptic error messages. The client was understandably frustrated, and the pressure was on to fix the issues as quickly as possible.

At first, I fell into the same old habits. I started tweaking the code, adding print statements, and making changes based on hunches. But nothing worked. In fact, I ended up making the problem worse by introducing new bugs. That's when a senior developer on the team pulled me aside and said something that stuck with me: "Debugging isn't about guessing—it's about gathering evidence." He showed me how to approach the problem systematically, and it completely changed the way I think about debugging.

The first step was to reproduce the issue consistently. This might sound obvious, but it's something I had often overlooked in my rush to fix things. If you can't reproduce a bug, you can't be sure you've fixed it. For the chat app, we set up a test environment that simulated the same conditions as the production server, including the high traffic that seemed to trigger the issues. Once we could reproduce the problem reliably, we started gathering data. We looked at the server logs, monitored resource usage, and traced the flow of messages through the system. Instead of guessing what might be wrong, we were building a clear picture of what was actually happening.

One of the most useful tools we used was a debugger. I had always thought of debuggers as something you only used for stepping through code line by line, but they're so much more than that. For the chat app, we used the debugger to inspect the state of the application at different points in time. We set breakpoints in the message-handling code and watched how the data changed as it moved through the system. This helped us pinpoint the exact moment where things were going wrong: a race condition in the code that caused messages to be dropped under heavy load. Once we understood the problem, fixing it was relatively straightforward.

That experience taught me the value of a systematic debugging approach, but it also made me aware of some common pitfalls that can make debugging harder than it needs to be. One of the biggest mistakes I used to make was assuming that the problem was in the code I had just written. It's natural to think that a bug must be related to your most recent changes, but that's not always the case. On one project, I spent hours trying to debug a feature I had just implemented, only to discover that the issue was caused by a bug in a third-party library we were using. If I had taken a step back and considered all the possibilities, I could have saved myself a lot of time and frustration.

Another common pitfall is jumping to conclusions without fully understanding the problem. I've seen developers (myself included) waste hours chasing the wrong issue because they assumed they knew what was causing it. For example, on one project, we were seeing intermittent crashes in a mobile app. Everyone assumed it was a memory leak, so we spent days profiling the app and optimizing memory usage. But the crashes didn't stop. It wasn't until we looked at the crash logs more closely that we realized the problem was actually a threading issue. If we had taken the time to analyze the evidence before jumping to conclusions, we could have solved the problem much faster.

One of the most frustrating aspects of debugging is the feedback loop—the time it takes to test a change and see if it fixes the problem. On some projects, this loop can be painfully long, especially if you have to rebuild the application or redeploy it to a server every time you make a change. I've worked on projects where the feedback loop was so slow that debugging even a simple issue could take hours. Over time, I've learned a few strategies for reducing the feedback loop and making the debugging process more efficient.

One of the most effective strategies is to isolate the problem as much as possible. For example, if you're debugging a function that's part of a larger system, try to extract it into a standalone script or test case. This allows you to focus on the specific issue without being distracted by the rest of the system. On one project, we were debugging a bug in a data processing pipeline that involved multiple services and databases. Instead of running the entire pipeline every time we made a change, we created a small test script that simulated the input and output of the problematic service. This reduced the feedback loop from several minutes to just a few seconds, which made it much easier to iterate on the code and find the root cause of the issue.

Another way to reduce the feedback loop is to use tools that allow you to make changes without restarting the application. For example, many modern development environments support hot reloading, which lets you update the code and see the changes immediately without restarting the server or rebuilding the application. On one project, we were debugging a web application with a particularly slow build process. By enabling hot reloading, we were able to test changes almost instantly, which saved us hours of time.

Logging is another powerful tool for reducing the feedback loop. By adding detailed log messages to your code, you can gather information about what's happening without having to stop and restart the application. On one project, we were debugging a bug in a background job that only occurred under certain conditions. Instead of trying to reproduce the issue manually, we added logging to track the state of the job at each step. This allowed us to see exactly where things were going wrong, without having to run the job over and over again.

Looking back, I realize that debugging is as much about mindset as it is about tools and techniques. It's about being patient, methodical, and willing to question your assumptions. It's about gathering evidence, analyzing the data, and understanding the problem before you try to fix it. And it's about learning from your mistakes so you can avoid them in the future.

The chat app, the mobile app, the data pipeline—each of these projects taught me something new about debugging. They taught me to approach problems systematically, to avoid common pitfalls, and to find ways to reduce the feedback loop. But perhaps the most important lesson I've learned is that debugging isn't just a technical skill—it's a mindset. It's about being curious, persistent, and willing to dig deep to find the root cause of a problem. And when you approach debugging with that mindset, it stops being a frustrating chore and becomes an opportunity to learn and grow as a developer.

CHAPTER EIGHT

Efficient Debugging and Maintenance

Identifying the Root Cause

I'll never forget the time I spent debugging a particularly elusive issue in a large e-commerce platform. The bug was reported by a customer who claimed that their shopping cart would randomly empty itself during checkout. At first, the team dismissed it as user error—maybe they had accidentally logged out or cleared their browser cache. But then more reports started coming in, and it became clear that this wasn't an isolated incident. The problem was real, and it was costing the company money. What followed was one of the most challenging debugging experiences of my career, but it also taught me some of the most valuable lessons about identifying the root cause of a problem.

The first step in tackling the issue was to gather as much information as possible. This is where log analysis and error monitoring became invaluable. At the time, the platform was already set up with a basic logging system, but the logs were scattered across multiple services and weren't very detailed. We had to sift through thousands of lines of logs, looking for anything that might explain why the shopping cart was being emptied. It was like searching for a needle in a haystack, and it quickly became clear that our logging system wasn't up to the task.

To make sense of the chaos, we started by centralizing the logs using a tool that aggregated them into a single dashboard. This made it much easier to search for patterns and correlations. For example, we noticed that the cart-emptying issue seemed to occur more frequently during peak traffic times. This was a crucial clue—it suggested that the problem might be related to how the system handled concurrent requests. But the logs alone weren't enough to pinpoint the exact cause. They gave us hints, but we needed more data.

That's when we turned to error monitoring tools. Unlike traditional logs, which require you to sift through raw data manually, error monitoring tools automatically capture and categorize errors as they occur. They also provide additional context, like the stack trace, user session data, and the exact conditions under which the error happened. By integrating one of these tools into the platform, we were able to see a clearer picture of what was going wrong. For example, we discovered that the cart-emptying issue was often preceded by a specific error in the session management service. This narrowed our focus and gave us a starting point for further investigation.

Once we had some clues, the next step was to reproduce the bug consistently. This is one of the most important—and often most frustrating—parts of debugging. If you can't reproduce a bug, you can't be sure you've fixed it. In this case, reproducing the issue was particularly challenging because it only seemed to happen under certain conditions, like high traffic or specific user actions. We couldn't just sit around waiting for it to happen again in production.

To tackle this, we set up a test environment that mimicked the production system as closely as possible. This included simulating high traffic by using load-testing tools to generate thousands of concurrent requests. We also wrote scripts to automate common user actions, like adding items to the cart, logging in and out, and proceeding to checkout. After several hours of testing, we finally managed to reproduce the issue. It turned out that under heavy load, the session management service was occasionally overwriting active sessions with stale data, causing the shopping cart to appear empty.

Reproducing the bug was a breakthrough, but it was only half the battle. The next step was to figure out why the session management service was behaving this way. This is where defensive coding techniques came into play. Defensive coding is all about anticipating potential problems and designing your code to handle them gracefully. It's not just about fixing bugs—it's about preventing them in the first place.

As we dug into the session management code, we realized that it wasn't designed to handle concurrent requests properly. The service used a shared in-memory data structure to store session data, but it didn't have any safeguards to prevent multiple requests from modifying the same session at the same time. This led to a classic race condition, where the outcome depended on the timing of the requests. Under normal conditions, the race condition was rare, but during peak traffic, it became much more likely.

To fix the issue, we implemented a locking mechanism to ensure that only one request could modify a session at a time. We also added more detailed logging to the session management service, so we could monitor its behavior and catch similar issues in the future. But we didn't stop there. We took a step back and looked at the system as a whole, asking ourselves: *What other parts of the code might be vulnerable to similar issues?* This led us to review and refactor several other services, applying defensive coding techniques to make them more robust.

For example, we added input validation to ensure that invalid data couldn't cause unexpected behavior. We also implemented timeouts and retries for external API calls, so the system wouldn't hang or crash if a third-party service was slow to respond. And we introduced circuit breakers to prevent cascading failures, where a problem in one part of the system could bring down the entire platform. These changes didn't just fix the immediate issue—they made the system more resilient overall.

Looking back, I realize that identifying the root cause of a problem is as much about mindset as it is about tools and techniques. It's about being curious, methodical, and willing to dig deep to understand what's really going on. It's about gathering evidence, reproducing the issue, and thinking critically about how the system is designed. And it's about learning from each bug you encounter, so you can write better, more reliable code in the future.

The shopping cart bug was a painful experience, but it also taught me some of the most valuable lessons of my career. It taught me the importance of good logging and error monitoring, not just for debugging but for understanding how the system behaves in the real world. It taught me the value of reproducing bugs consistently, even when it's difficult or time-consuming. And it taught me the power of defensive coding techniques, not just for fixing problems but for preventing them in the first place.

Since then, I've applied these lessons to every project I've worked on. Whether I'm building a small app or a large-scale system, I always start by setting up good logging and error monitoring. I make sure I can reproduce any issues that arise, and I use defensive coding techniques to anticipate and handle potential problems. These practices don't just make debugging easier—they make the entire development process more efficient and less stressful.

At the end of the day, debugging isn't just about fixing bugs—it's about understanding your system and making it better. It's about taking the time to identify the root cause of a problem, rather than just treating the symptoms. And when you approach debugging with that mindset, it stops being a frustrating chore and becomes an opportunity to learn, grow, and build better software.

Maintenance Strategies

I once worked on a project for a logistics company that had been using the same software system for over a decade. The system was critical to their operations, handling everything from inventory management to shipment tracking. But it was also a mess. The codebase was bloated, riddled with hacks and workarounds, and barely documented. Every time a new feature was requested, it felt like walking into a minefield. Fixing one bug would inevitably break something else, and adding new functionality often required days of untangling old code just to figure out how it worked. It was a classic case of technical debt, and it taught me a lot about the importance of effective maintenance strategies.

One of the first things I learned on that project was the value of refactoring old code. At first, I was hesitant to touch anything that wasn't directly related to the task at hand. The code was so fragile that even small changes could have unintended consequences, and I didn't want to make things worse. But over time, I realized that avoiding the problem wasn't a sustainable strategy. If we wanted to make the system easier to work with, we had to start cleaning it up.

Refactoring isn't about rewriting everything from scratch—it's about making incremental improvements to the existing code. On the logistics system, we started by identifying the most problematic areas of the codebase. For example, there was a function that calculated shipping costs, but it was over 500 lines long and filled with nested conditionals that made it almost impossible to understand. Every time we needed to update the shipping rules, we had to spend hours deciphering the logic.

To refactor the function, we broke it down into smaller, more manageable pieces. Instead of one monolithic block of code, we created separate functions for each type of shipping rule. We also added comments and unit tests to ensure that the refactored code behaved the same way as the original. The process wasn't quick or easy, but it paid off in the long run. The new code was not only easier to read and maintain but also less prone to bugs. And because we tackled the refactoring incrementally, we were able to make progress without disrupting the rest of the system.

Of course, not all maintenance work involves refactoring. Sometimes, you're dealing with legacy systems that are so outdated that they can't be salvaged. On another project, I worked with a team that was tasked with replacing a legacy billing system for a telecommunications company. The old system had been built in the 1990s and was written in a programming language that none of us were familiar with. It was slow, unreliable, and couldn't handle the company's growing customer base. But it was also deeply embedded in the company's operations, and replacing it was a massive undertaking.

One of the biggest challenges with legacy systems is balancing the need for stability with the need for change. On the one hand, you don't want to disrupt critical business processes by making changes too quickly. On the other hand, you can't afford to let the system stagnate. For the billing system, we took a phased approach. Instead of replacing the entire system at once, we started by building a new system alongside the old one. We migrated one feature at a time, testing each change thoroughly before moving on to the next. This allowed us to minimize risk while gradually modernizing the system.

Working with legacy systems also taught me the importance of understanding the business context. It's easy to look at an old system and think, *Why don't we just throw this away and start over?* But legacy systems often contain years of accumulated knowledge and business logic that can't be easily replicated. On the billing system project, we spent weeks interviewing the original developers (some of whom had retired but were brought back as consultants) and poring over old documentation to understand how the system worked. This knowledge was invaluable when it came time to design the new system.

Speaking of documentation, one of the most important lessons I've learned about maintenance is the value of good documentation and knowledge transfer. On too many projects, documentation is treated as an afterthought, something you do if you have time at the end of the project. But when it comes to maintenance, documentation is often the difference between success and failure.

I once joined a team that was responsible for maintaining a large web application. The original developers had all left the company, and there was almost no documentation. The codebase was full of cryptic variable names and unexplained hacks, and every bug fix felt like solving a puzzle with half the pieces missing. It was a frustrating experience, and it made me realize how much time and effort could have been saved if the original developers had taken the time to document their work.

Good documentation doesn't have to be complicated. It's not about writing a novel—it's about providing enough context to help the next person understand what the code is doing and why. On one project, we made it a rule to include a brief comment at the top of every file, explaining its purpose and any important details. We also created a shared knowledge base where we documented common patterns, troubleshooting tips, and the reasoning behind major design decisions. This not only made it easier for new team members to get up to speed but also reduced the amount of time we spent answering the same questions over and over again.

Knowledge transfer is another critical aspect of maintenance, especially when team members leave or new people join. On one project, we implemented a "buddy system" where every developer was paired with someone else who was familiar with their work. This ensured that no one person became a single point of failure. We also held regular knowledge-sharing sessions where team members could present what they were working on and share any lessons they had learned. These sessions weren't just about transferring knowledge—they were also an opportunity to build a culture of collaboration and continuous learning.

Looking back, I realize that maintenance is one of the most challenging—and rewarding—aspects of software development. It's not as glamorous as building something new, but it's just as important. Whether you're refactoring old code, working with legacy systems, or documenting your work for the next person, maintenance is about taking responsibility for the long-term health of the system. It's about recognizing that software isn't static—it evolves over time, and it's up to us to ensure that it remains reliable, maintainable, and useful.

The logistics system, the billing system, the web application—each of these projects taught me something new about maintenance. They taught me the value of refactoring, not just to fix problems but to make the code easier to work with. They taught me the challenges and opportunities of working with legacy systems, and the importance of understanding the business context. And they taught me the power of documentation and knowledge transfer, not just for the sake of efficiency but for building a culture of shared responsibility.

At the end of the day, maintenance isn't just about fixing bugs or adding features—it's about ensuring that the software continues to deliver value over time. It's about leaving the codebase better than you found it, so that the next person can build on your work instead of struggling to understand it. And when you approach maintenance with that mindset, it stops being a chore and becomes an opportunity to make a lasting impact.

Continuous Improvement

One of the most memorable projects I ever worked on was a large-scale SaaS platform for a retail company. The platform handled everything from inventory management to customer analytics, and it was a critical part of their business. One day, during a major holiday sale, the system went down. Completely. Orders weren't being processed, customers couldn't check out, and the company was losing thousands of dollars every minute. The team scrambled to bring the system back online, and after hours of frantic debugging, we managed to patch the issue. But the experience left everyone shaken. What had gone wrong? Could we have prevented it? And how could we ensure it wouldn't happen again?

That incident was my first real introduction to the concept of post-mortems and blameless retrospectives. After the system was stabilized, the team gathered to analyze what had happened. The goal wasn't to point fingers or assign blame—it was to understand the root cause of the failure and identify ways to improve. We started by documenting the timeline of events: when the issue was first reported, what actions were taken, and how the problem was ultimately resolved. This helped us piece together a clear picture of what had gone wrong.

It turned out that the outage was caused by a combination of factors. A recent update had introduced a subtle bug in the database query logic, which only became apparent under heavy load. At the same time, our monitoring system hadn't been configured to alert us to the early signs of trouble, so we didn't realize there was a problem until the system was already failing. These were preventable issues, but they highlighted gaps in our processes that we hadn't addressed before.

The most valuable part of the post-mortem was the discussion about how to prevent similar incidents in the future. We decided to implement stricter code review processes to catch potential issues before they made it to production. We also improved our monitoring and alerting systems, setting up thresholds to detect unusual patterns in traffic or resource usage. And we created a playbook for handling outages, so that if something like this happened again, we'd be better prepared to respond quickly and effectively.

What I appreciated most about the post-mortem was the blameless approach. Instead of focusing on who had made the mistake, we focused on what we could learn from it. This created a culture of trust and collaboration, where team members felt safe admitting their mistakes and sharing their ideas for improvement. Over time, these post-mortems became a regular part of our workflow, not just for major incidents but for any significant issue. They helped us identify patterns, refine our processes, and continuously improve as a team.

Another key aspect of continuous improvement is versioning and release management. On the same SaaS platform, we initially had a very ad-hoc approach to releases. Features were deployed as soon as they were ready, often without much coordination or planning. This led to a lot of problems. For example, one developer might deploy a new feature that inadvertently broke another part of the system, or a bug fix might introduce a regression because it hadn't been tested thoroughly. It became clear that we needed a more structured approach.

We started by adopting semantic versioning, a system for numbering releases based on the type of changes they include. For example, a major version (e.g., 2.0.0) would indicate breaking changes, a minor version (e.g., 2.1.0) would indicate new features, and a patch version (e.g., 2.1.1) would indicate bug fixes. This made it easier for everyone—developers, testers, and even stakeholders—to understand the scope of each release and plan accordingly.

We also introduced a release management process that included multiple stages: development, testing, staging, and production. Each stage had its own set of checks and balances. For example, before a release could move from testing to staging, it had to pass a suite of automated tests and a round of manual testing. And before it could move to production, it had to be reviewed and approved by a release manager. This process added some overhead, but it significantly reduced the risk of deploying buggy or incomplete code.

One of the most important lessons I learned about release management is the value of small, incremental changes. On one project, we made the mistake of bundling too many changes into a single release. The release included several new features, a major refactor, and a handful of bug fixes. When things went wrong, it was almost impossible to pinpoint the cause because there were so many variables. After that, we started breaking releases into smaller, more manageable chunks. This made it easier to test, debug, and roll back changes if necessary.

Planning for future enhancements is another critical part of continuous improvement. On the SaaS platform, we often found ourselves reacting to immediate needs—fixing bugs, adding features requested by stakeholders, or addressing performance issues. But this reactive approach made it difficult to think strategically about the long-term direction of the platform. We realized that if we wanted to build a system that could evolve and scale over time, we needed to start planning for the future.

One of the first steps we took was to create a product roadmap. This wasn't a rigid plan—it was a high-level outline of where we wanted the platform to go over the next six months to a year. The roadmap included major features, technical improvements, and business goals, and it was updated regularly based on feedback from stakeholders and users. Having a roadmap helped us prioritize our work and ensure that we were making progress toward our long-term goals, not just putting out fires.

We also started thinking more carefully about scalability and maintainability. For example, when designing new features, we asked questions like: *How will this feature perform under heavy load? How easy will it be to extend or modify in the future?* On one occasion, we were asked to add a new reporting feature that required querying large amounts of data. Instead of building the feature directly into the platform, we created a separate reporting service that could be scaled independently. This not only improved performance but also made it easier to add new reports in the future.

Another important aspect of planning for future enhancements is involving the entire team in the process. On one project, we held regular brainstorming sessions where developers, designers, and stakeholders could share their ideas for improving the system. These sessions weren't just about generating new ideas—they were also an opportunity to identify pain points and discuss how to address them. For example, one developer pointed out that our deployment process was too slow and suggested automating more of the steps. Another team member suggested creating a style guide to ensure consistency across the platform. These ideas might not have been part of the original roadmap, but they were valuable contributions that helped us improve the system over time.

Looking back, I realize that continuous improvement isn't just about fixing problems or adding features—it's about creating a culture of learning and growth. It's about being proactive, not reactive, and constantly looking for ways to do things better. Whether it's through post-mortems, versioning, or planning for the future, continuous improvement is what allows a system to evolve and thrive over time.

The SaaS platform, the retail system, the reporting service—each of these projects taught me something new about continuous improvement. They taught me the value of learning from mistakes, the importance of structured release management, and the power of planning for the future. But perhaps the most important lesson I've learned is that continuous improvement isn't just a technical practice—it's a mindset. It's about embracing change, seeking feedback, and always striving to do better. And when you approach your work with that mindset, you're not just maintaining a system—you're building something that can stand the test of time.

CHAPTER NINE

Time Management and Productivity

Prioritizing Tasks and Projects

Time management is one of those skills that every developer knows they need but few truly master. Early in my career, I struggled with it constantly. I'd start my day with a long to-do list, full of good intentions, only to find myself at the end of the day wondering where all the time had gone. I'd spend hours putting out fires, jumping between tasks, and responding to interruptions, but the most important work—the work that really moved the needle—always seemed to get pushed to the side. It wasn't until I started learning how to prioritize effectively that I began to feel in control of my time.

One of the most transformative tools I discovered was the **Urgent vs. Important Matrix**, also known as the Eisenhower Matrix. The concept is simple but powerful: every task can be categorized as either urgent or important, and understanding the difference is key to managing your time effectively. Urgent tasks demand immediate attention—they're the emails, the last-minute bug fixes, the client calls. Important tasks, on the other hand, are the ones that contribute to your long-term goals, like planning a project, learning a new skill, or writing clean, maintainable code. The problem is that urgent tasks often feel more pressing, so they tend to take over your day, leaving little room for the important work.

I remember one project where this distinction became painfully clear. I was working on a new feature for a mobile app, and the deadline was tight. Every day, I'd come into the office with a plan to focus on the feature, but I'd quickly get derailed by urgent tasks—fixing bugs in the existing app, responding to emails from the client, helping a teammate troubleshoot an issue. By the end of the week, I'd barely made any progress on the feature, and the deadline was looming. That's when my manager introduced me to the matrix.

We sat down together and listed all my tasks for the week, then categorized them into four quadrants:

1. **Urgent and Important:** These were the tasks that couldn't wait, like fixing a critical bug that was affecting users.
2. **Important but Not Urgent:** This included the feature I was supposed to be working on—it wasn't due immediately, but it was critical to the project's success.
3. **Urgent but Not Important:** These were the distractions, like non-critical emails and requests that could have been delegated.
4. **Neither Urgent nor Important:** These were the time-wasters, like checking social media or getting caught up in unnecessary meetings.

Seeing my tasks laid out like this was a wake-up call. I realized I was spending most of my time in the first and third quadrants, dealing with urgent tasks, while the important work in the second quadrant was being neglected. From that point on, I made a conscious effort to prioritize the important-but-not-urgent tasks. I blocked out time on my calendar to work on the feature, turned off email notifications, and politely declined or delegated tasks that weren't a good use of my time. It wasn't easy at first—I had to fight the urge to respond to every interruption—but the results were worth it. By the end of the week, I had made significant progress on the feature, and I felt a sense of accomplishment that had been missing before.

Another strategy that helped me prioritize my work was adopting **Agile methodologies and sprints**. Before Agile, the projects I worked on often felt chaotic. We'd start with a vague plan, then spend weeks or months trying to execute it, only to realize halfway through that we were off track. Deadlines would slip, priorities would shift, and the team would end up scrambling to deliver something—anything—by the end of the project. It was stressful and demoralizing, and it often felt like we were working harder, not smarter.

Agile changed all that. Instead of trying to plan everything upfront, we started breaking our work into smaller, more manageable chunks called sprints. Each sprint lasted two weeks, and at the beginning of each sprint, we'd sit down as a team to prioritize our tasks. We used a backlog to keep track of all the work that needed to be done, and we'd pull the most important tasks into the sprint. This forced us to focus on what really mattered and gave us a clear sense of direction.

One of the things I love about sprints is the built-in feedback loop. At the end of each sprint, we'd hold a retrospective to discuss what went well, what didn't, and what we could improve. On one project, for example, we realized during a retrospective that we were spending too much time on low-priority tasks because we hadn't been clear about our goals for the sprint. In the next sprint, we made a point to define our priorities more explicitly, and it made a huge difference. We were able to deliver a key feature on time, and the team felt more focused and productive.

Agile also taught me the importance of breaking tasks into smaller pieces. On one project, I was assigned to build a complex reporting feature for a web app. At first, the task felt overwhelming—it was hard to know where to start. But by breaking it down into smaller tasks, like designing the database schema, writing the API endpoints, and building the front-end interface, I was able to make steady progress. Each small win gave me a sense of momentum, and by the end of the sprint, the feature was complete.

Of course, even with the best prioritization strategies, interruptions and task switching are inevitable. I used to think I was good at multitasking—I'd jump between coding, answering emails, and attending meetings without missing a beat. But over time, I realized that task switching was killing my productivity. Every time I switched from one task to another, it took me several minutes to get back into the flow of what I was doing. And the more I switched, the more fragmented my day became.

One of the most disruptive interruptions I ever experienced was during a critical bug fix for a production system. I was deep in the code, trying to trace the root cause of the issue, when a teammate tapped me on the shoulder to ask for help with a completely unrelated problem. I spent 15 minutes helping them, then tried to get back to the bug fix, only to realize I had lost my train of thought. It took me another 20 minutes just to get back to where I was before the interruption. By the end of the day, I had made far less progress than I should have.

To handle interruptions more effectively, I started setting boundaries. For example, I blocked out "focus time" on my calendar, during which I wouldn't check email or take meetings. I also started using a technique called "timeboxing," where I set a timer for a specific amount of time and focused on a single task until the timer went off. This helped me stay on track and resist the urge to switch tasks. And when teammates came to me with questions, I politely asked if it could wait until I finished what I was working on. Most of the time, they were happy to wait, and I was able to stay focused.

Another strategy that helped was creating a system for managing interruptions. On one project, our team set up a shared Slack channel for non-urgent questions and updates. Instead of interrupting each other throughout the day, we posted our questions in the channel and checked it during designated times. This reduced the number of interruptions and allowed everyone to focus on their work without feeling disconnected from the team.

Looking back, I realize that prioritizing tasks and projects isn't just about managing your time—it's about managing your energy and attention. It's about recognizing that not all tasks are created equal and focusing on the ones that truly matter. It's about creating systems and habits that help you stay on track, even in the face of distractions. And it's about learning from your mistakes and continuously improving your approach.

The mobile app feature, the Agile sprints, the production bug fix—each of these experiences taught me something new about prioritization. They taught me the value of focusing on what's important, the power of breaking work into smaller pieces, and the importance of setting boundaries to protect my time and attention. But perhaps the most important lesson I've learned is that prioritization isn't just a skill—it's a mindset. It's about being intentional with your time and making choices that align with your goals. And when you approach your work with that mindset, you'll find that you're not just getting more done—you're getting the right things done.

Work-Life Balance

When I first started working in tech, I was thrilled by the fast pace and the endless opportunities to learn. I'd stay up late debugging code, spend weekends experimenting with new frameworks, and jump at the chance to take on extra projects. I thought this was what it meant to be passionate about your work. But after a few years, I hit a wall. I was constantly exhausted, my creativity had dried up, and I started dreading the very work I used to love. It took me a long time to realize that I was burned out—and even longer to figure out how to fix it.

Burnout is a common problem in tech, where the pressure to deliver, the lure of constant innovation, and the always-on culture can make it hard to step away. One of the first strategies I learned to combat burnout was the importance of taking breaks—not just during the day, but over the course of a project or even a career. Early in my career, I worked on a high-stakes project for a startup. The deadlines were tight, and the team was small, so we all put in long hours to get the product ready for launch. At first, the adrenaline kept me going, but as the weeks dragged on, I started to feel the effects. I was irritable, I couldn't focus, and I started making mistakes that I wouldn't normally make.

One day, my manager pulled me aside and said, "You need to take a day off." I resisted at first—I didn't want to let the team down—but eventually, I agreed. I spent the day hiking in the mountains, completely disconnected from work. When I came back, I felt like a different person. I was more focused, more creative, and more productive. That experience taught me that rest isn't a luxury—it's a necessity. Now, I make a point to schedule regular breaks, even during busy periods. Whether it's a 10-minute walk during the day or a long weekend away from my computer, these breaks help me recharge and stay engaged with my work.

Another strategy that helped me combat burnout was learning to say no. In tech, there's always more work to do—more features to build, more bugs to fix, more opportunities to explore. It's easy to fall into the trap of saying yes to everything, but this is a surefire way to overextend yourself. I learned this the hard way on a project where I agreed to take on extra responsibilities, thinking I could handle it all. But as the workload piled up, I started to feel overwhelmed. I was working late every night, and my personal life was suffering. Eventually, I had to admit that I couldn't do it all. I sat down with my manager and explained the situation. To my surprise, they were understanding and helped me reprioritize my tasks. That experience taught me that saying no isn't a sign of weakness—it's a way to protect your time and energy so you can focus on what really matters.

Setting boundaries is another critical part of maintaining work-life balance, especially in a 24/7 world where the lines between work and personal life are increasingly blurred. I remember one job where I felt like I was always on call. Emails would come in at all hours, and there was an unspoken expectation that I'd respond immediately. At first, I went along with it, but over time, I started to feel resentful. I'd be out with friends or spending time with my family, and I'd get pulled back into work. It felt like I could never fully disconnect.

Eventually, I realized that I needed to set boundaries. I started by turning off email notifications on my phone and setting specific times to check my inbox. I also made it clear to my team that I wouldn't be available outside of work hours unless it was an emergency. At first, I worried that this would make me seem uncommitted, but the opposite happened. By setting boundaries, I was able to be more present and focused during work hours, which made me a better teammate and a more effective developer. And when I wasn't working, I could fully relax and recharge, knowing that I'd set clear expectations with my team.

One of the most important lessons I've learned about work-life balance is that it's not just about managing your time—it's about taking care of your physical and mental well-being. Early in my career, I thought I could power through anything as long as I worked hard enough. I'd skip meals, stay up late, and spend hours hunched over my computer without taking a break. But over time, I started to notice the toll it was taking on my body and mind. I was constantly tired, I had frequent headaches, and I felt anxious and stressed all the time.

It wasn't until I started prioritizing my health that I began to feel like myself again. One of the first changes I made was to incorporate exercise into my routine. At first, it was hard to find the time, but I started small—just a 20-minute walk during lunch or a quick workout in the morning. Over time, I noticed a huge difference. I had more energy, I slept better, and I felt less stressed. Exercise became a way to clear my mind and reset, and it helped me approach my work with a fresh perspective.

Another change I made was to pay more attention to my mental health. In tech, there's often a stigma around admitting that you're struggling, but I've learned that asking for help is one of the bravest things you can do. On one particularly stressful project, I started seeing a therapist to help me manage my anxiety. They taught me techniques like mindfulness and deep breathing, which I still use today when I'm feeling overwhelmed. I also started journaling as a way to process my thoughts and reflect on my day. These practices have helped me stay grounded, even during the most challenging times.

One of the most surprising things I've learned about work-life balance is how much it's influenced by the culture of the team or company you work for. On one project, I worked with a team that had a healthy approach to work-life balance. The managers encouraged us to take breaks, respected our boundaries, and celebrated our achievements without expecting us to sacrifice our personal lives. As a result, the team was not only happier but also more productive. We were able to deliver high-quality work without burning out, and we felt supported and valued as individuals.

On another project, the culture was the complete opposite. There was constant pressure to work long hours, and anyone who left the office on time was seen as uncommitted. The team was exhausted, morale was low, and turnover was high. That experience taught me the importance of advocating for a healthy work-life balance, not just for myself but for the entire team. Whether it's encouraging teammates to take breaks, speaking up when the workload becomes unsustainable, or leading by example by setting boundaries, we all have a role to play in creating a culture that values balance.

Looking back, I realize that work-life balance isn't something you achieve once and then forget about—it's an ongoing process. It requires self-awareness, discipline, and a willingness to make changes when things aren't working. It's about recognizing that your time and energy are finite resources and using them wisely. And it's about understanding that taking care of yourself isn't just good for you—it's good for your work, your team, and the people who depend on you.

The startup project, the always-on job, the supportive team—each of these experiences taught me something new about work-life balance. They taught me the importance of taking breaks, setting boundaries, and prioritizing my physical and mental well-being. But perhaps the most important lesson I've learned is that work-life balance isn't just about managing your time—it's about living your life in a way that's sustainable, fulfilling, and true to your values. And when you approach your work with that mindset, you'll find that you're not just more productive—you're happier, healthier, and more engaged with the things that matter most.

Leveraging Tools and Automation

When I first started working as a developer, I thought productivity was all about working harder and putting in more hours. I'd keep a mental list of tasks, jump between projects, and rely on sheer willpower to stay organized. But as the complexity of my work grew, I started to feel overwhelmed. Deadlines slipped, important tasks fell through the cracks, and I spent more time reacting to problems than proactively solving them. It wasn't until I started leveraging tools and automation that I realized productivity isn't about working harder—it's about working smarter.

One of the first tools that transformed the way I worked was a task management platform. At the time, I was juggling multiple projects, each with its own set of deadlines, deliverables, and stakeholders. I'd scribble notes on sticky pads, send myself reminder emails, and try to keep everything straight in my head. Inevitably, I'd forget something—a meeting, a bug fix, or a follow-up with a teammate—and I'd have to scramble to catch up. It was stressful and inefficient, and I knew I needed a better system.

That's when I discovered task management platforms like Trello and Asana. At first, I was skeptical—did I really need another tool? But once I started using them, I realized how much easier they made my life. I could create boards for each project, break tasks into smaller steps, and assign deadlines to keep myself accountable. For example, on one project, I was responsible for building a new feature for a web app. Instead of trying to tackle the entire feature at once, I used a task management tool to break it down into smaller tasks: designing the database schema, writing the API endpoints, and building the front-end interface. Each task had its own deadline, and I could track my progress visually as I moved tasks from "To Do" to "In Progress" to "Done." This not only helped me stay organized but also gave me a sense of accomplishment as I completed each step.

Task management tools also made collaboration much easier. On one project, I worked with a distributed team spread across multiple time zones. Before we started using a collaboration platform, communication was chaotic. We'd send emails back and forth, lose track of who was responsible for what, and waste time duplicating work. But once we started using a shared task management tool, everything changed. We could assign tasks to specific team members, leave comments to clarify requirements, and track progress in real time. For example, when a teammate in another time zone finished their part of a task, they'd update the status in the tool, and I'd get a notification when I logged in the next morning. This seamless handoff saved us hours of back-and-forth and made the entire team more productive.

While task management tools helped me stay organized, automation was what really took my productivity to the next level. As a developer, I often found myself doing the same repetitive tasks over and over again: setting up development environments, running tests, deploying code, and so on. These tasks weren't difficult, but they were time-consuming and prone to error. I started to wonder: *Is there a way to automate this?*

One of the first tasks I automated was setting up a development environment for a new project. At the time, our team was working on multiple projects, each with its own dependencies and configurations. Every time I started a new project, I'd spend hours installing libraries, configuring settings, and troubleshooting issues. It was tedious, and I often made mistakes that caused problems down the line. To solve this, I created a script that automated the entire process. With a single command, the script would clone the repository, install the necessary dependencies, and configure the environment. What used to take hours now took minutes, and I could start coding right away.

Another area where automation made a huge difference was testing. On one project, we had a large codebase with hundreds of unit tests, integration tests, and end-to-end tests. Running the tests manually was time-consuming, and it was easy to forget to run them before pushing code to the repository. This led to bugs slipping into production, which caused headaches for the team and frustration for our users. To address this, we set up a continuous integration (CI) pipeline that automatically ran the tests every time someone pushed code to the repository. If any tests failed, the pipeline would block the code from being merged until the issue was resolved. This not only saved us time but also improved the quality of our code and gave us confidence that our changes wouldn't break anything.

Automation isn't just about saving time—it's also about reducing cognitive load. On one project, I was responsible for deploying updates to a production server. The process involved several steps: pulling the latest code from the repository, building the application, running tests, and restarting the server. Each step had to be done in a specific order, and if I missed a step, it could cause problems for our users. To make things easier, I wrote a deployment script that automated the entire process. Instead of worrying about whether I'd forgotten something, I could run the script and let it handle everything for me. This freed up my mental energy to focus on more important tasks, like debugging issues or planning new features.

While tools and automation helped me stay organized and save time, I also wanted to measure my productivity to see where I could improve. At first, I wasn't sure how to do this—how do you measure something as intangible as productivity? But then I discovered analytics tools that could track how I was spending my time. For example, one tool I used analyzed my calendar and email activity to show me how much time I was spending in meetings, responding to emails, and working on focused tasks. The results were eye-opening. I realized that I was spending far more time in meetings than I thought, which left me with little time for deep, focused work.

To address this, I started blocking out "focus time" on my calendar and declining meetings that weren't essential. I also set aside specific times to check email, rather than letting it interrupt me throughout the day. These small changes made a big difference—I was able to spend more time on the tasks that really mattered, and I felt less stressed and more in control of my time.

On another project, I used a code analytics tool to measure the quality of our codebase. The tool provided metrics like code complexity, test coverage, and the number of bugs reported over time. This helped us identify areas where we could improve, like refactoring overly complex code or writing more tests. For example, we noticed that one part of the codebase had a high bug rate compared to the rest of the system. By analyzing the metrics, we realized that the code was poorly documented and difficult to understand, which made it prone to errors. We spent a sprint refactoring and documenting the code, and the bug rate dropped significantly.

One of the most valuable lessons I've learned about productivity is that it's not just about working faster—it's about working smarter. Tools and automation can help you save time, reduce errors, and focus on what really matters, but they're not a magic solution. You still need to be intentional about how you use them and make sure they align with your goals. For example, on one project, we started using a new collaboration tool that promised to streamline communication. But instead of making us more productive, it became a distraction—team members spent more time chatting in the tool than actually working. We eventually realized that the problem wasn't the tool itself—it was how we were using it. By setting clear guidelines for when and how to use the tool, we were able to get the benefits without the downsides.

Looking back, I realize that leveraging tools and automation isn't just about saving time—it's about creating systems that support your work and help you achieve your goals. Whether it's a task management platform that keeps you organized, a script that automates repetitive tasks, or an analytics tool that helps you measure and improve your productivity, these tools can make a huge difference. But the key is to use them thoughtfully and intentionally, always asking yourself: *How can I work smarter, not harder?*

The task management boards, the deployment scripts, the productivity analytics—each of these tools taught me something new about how to manage my time and energy. They taught me the value of organization, the power of automation, and the importance of measuring and improving my work. But perhaps the most important lesson I've learned is that productivity isn't just about getting more done—it's about getting the right things done, in a way that's sustainable and fulfilling. And when you approach your work with that mindset, you'll find that the tools and systems you use aren't just helping you work—they're helping you thrive.

CHAPTER TEN

TEAM COLLABORATION AND COMMUNICATION

Building Trust Within the Team

I'll never forget the first time I joined a team that truly felt like a cohesive unit. It was a small group of developers working on a healthcare platform, and from the outside, it didn't seem like anything special. But as I got to know the team, I realized there was something different about the way they worked together. They trusted each other completely. They weren't afraid to ask for help, admit mistakes, or challenge each other's ideas. It was the kind of environment where everyone felt safe to contribute, and as a result, the team was not only productive but also genuinely enjoyable to be a part of. That experience taught me that trust isn't just a nice-to-have in a team—it's the foundation of everything.

One of the most important ways to build trust within a team is through **open communication practices.** On that healthcare project, we had a daily stand-up meeting where everyone shared what they were working on, what challenges they were facing, and what help they needed. At first, I was hesitant to speak up—I didn't want to admit that I was struggling with a particular task or that I didn't understand something. But as I listened to my teammates, I noticed that they were completely honest about their own challenges. One developer admitted that they had accidentally introduced a bug that caused a major issue in production. Instead of blaming them, the team rallied around to fix the problem and figure out how to prevent it from happening again. That level of openness was contagious, and it made me feel safe to share my own struggles.

Over time, I realized that open communication isn't just about being honest—it's about creating an environment where honesty is encouraged and rewarded. On another project, I worked with a team where communication was much more guarded. People were afraid to admit mistakes or ask questions because they didn't want to appear incompetent. As a result, problems festered, and the team struggled to make progress. That experience taught me the importance of leading by example. When I became a team lead, I made a point to be transparent about my own mistakes and to ask for feedback regularly. I'd say things like, "I'm not sure if this is the best approach—what do you think?" or "I made a mistake here, but here's how I'm planning to fix it." By modeling open communication, I found that others were more willing to do the same, and the team became much more collaborative as a result.

Another key ingredient in building trust is **empathy and emotional intelligence**. On one project, I worked with a developer who was incredibly talented but also very quiet. They rarely spoke up in meetings, and when they did, their ideas were often dismissed or overlooked. I could tell they were frustrated, but I didn't know how to help. One day, I decided to have a one-on-one conversation with them. I asked how they were feeling about the project and whether there was anything I could do to support them. At first, they were hesitant to open up, but eventually, they shared that they felt undervalued and excluded from the decision-making process. They had great ideas but didn't feel confident enough to speak up in front of the whole team.

That conversation was a turning point. I realized that building trust isn't just about creating a safe environment—it's also about understanding and addressing the unique needs of each team member. After our conversation, I started making a conscious effort to include them in discussions and to highlight their contributions in meetings. For example, if they shared an idea with me privately, I'd say something like, "That's a great idea—why don't you bring it up in the next meeting?" or "I think [their name] had a really interesting perspective on this—can you share it with the group?" Over time, their confidence grew, and they became a much more active participant in the team. That experience taught me that empathy isn't just about being kind—it's about taking the time to understand where someone is coming from and finding ways to support them.

Empathy also plays a crucial role in resolving conflicts, which are inevitable in any team. On one project, I worked with two developers who had very different working styles. One was meticulous and detail-oriented, while the other was fast-paced and focused on getting things done quickly. Their approaches often clashed, and it led to tension in the team. For example, the detail-oriented developer would get frustrated when the other developer pushed code that wasn't fully tested, while the fast-paced developer felt like the other was slowing them down with unnecessary nitpicking. The tension eventually boiled over into a heated argument during a team meeting, and it was clear that something needed to be done.

As the team lead, I knew it was my responsibility to address the conflict. I started by having one-on-one conversations with each developer to understand their perspectives. I listened without judgment and tried to empathize with their frustrations. The detail-oriented developer explained that they cared deeply about quality and didn't want to release anything that might cause problems for users. The fast-paced developer, on the other hand, felt pressure to meet deadlines and didn't want to get bogged down in endless discussions about minor details. Both perspectives were valid, and I realized that the conflict wasn't about who was right or wrong—it was about finding a way to balance their priorities.

In our next team meeting, I facilitated a discussion to address the conflict. I started by acknowledging the tension and emphasizing that we were all on the same team, working toward the same goals. Then, I asked each developer to share their perspective, and I encouraged the rest of the team to listen without interrupting. Once everyone had a chance to speak, we brainstormed ways to address the underlying issues. For example, we agreed to set clearer expectations for code reviews, so that the fast-paced developer wouldn't feel like they were being held up unnecessarily. We also decided to prioritize critical tasks more explicitly, so that the detail-oriented developer could focus their energy on the areas that mattered most. By the end of the meeting, the tension had eased, and the team had a plan for moving forward.

That experience taught me that **conflict resolution** isn't about avoiding disagreements—it's about addressing them in a constructive way. One of the most effective techniques I've learned is to focus on the problem, not the person. For example, instead of saying, "You're always rushing and making mistakes," you might say, "I've noticed that some of the recent code changes have introduced bugs—how can we work together to prevent this in the future?" This shifts the conversation from blame to collaboration and makes it easier to find a solution.

Another important technique is to create space for open dialogue. On one project, I worked with a team that held regular "retrospectives" to reflect on what was working well and what could be improved. These meetings weren't just about processes—they were also an opportunity to address interpersonal issues in a safe and supportive environment. For example, if someone felt like their ideas weren't being heard, they could bring it up during the retrospective, and the team could discuss ways to improve communication. By making conflict resolution a regular part of our workflow, we were able to address issues before they escalated and build stronger relationships as a team.

Looking back, I realize that building trust within a team isn't something that happens overnight—it's an ongoing process that requires effort, empathy, and a commitment to open communication. The healthcare project, the quiet developer, the clashing working styles—each of these experiences taught me something new about what it takes to create a trusting and collaborative environment. They taught me the importance of being honest and transparent, of taking the time to understand and support each team member, and of addressing conflicts in a constructive way.

But perhaps the most important lesson I've learned is that trust isn't just a nice-to-have—it's the foundation of everything. When a team trusts each other, they're more willing to take risks, share ideas, and work together to solve problems. They're more resilient in the face of challenges and more motivated to achieve their goals. And when you're part of a team like that, work doesn't just feel like work—it feels like something bigger, something meaningful. And that's the kind of team I strive to build every day.

Effective Meetings and Brainstorming

Meetings are often seen as a necessary evil in the workplace. I've been in my fair share of meetings that felt like a waste of time—long, meandering discussions with no clear purpose, where everyone left more confused than when they arrived. But I've also been part of meetings that were energizing and productive, where ideas flowed freely, decisions were made, and everyone left with a clear sense of direction. The difference between the two often comes down to one thing: preparation. Over the years, I've learned that effective meetings don't just happen—they're carefully planned and executed. And when done right, they can be one of the most powerful tools for collaboration and innovation.

One of the most important lessons I've learned is the value of **agenda-driven meetings.** Early in my career, I worked on a project where the team held weekly status meetings. These meetings were supposed to help us stay aligned, but they often felt like a waste of time. There was no agenda, so we'd spend the first 10 minutes figuring out what to talk about. Conversations would drift off-topic, and by the end of the hour, we hadn't accomplished much. Frustrated, I suggested that we start using an agenda to structure our discussions. At first, it was a simple list of topics we wanted to cover, but over time, we refined it to include specific goals for each item. For example, instead of "Discuss feature X," the agenda might say, "Decide on the implementation approach for feature X." This small change made a huge difference. The meetings became more focused, and we were able to accomplish in 30 minutes what used to take an hour.

I've also found that sharing the agenda in advance is a great way to make meetings more effective. On one project, I worked with a distributed team spread across multiple time zones. To make the most of our limited overlap, we started sending out the agenda a day before each meeting. This gave everyone a chance to prepare and think about the topics we'd be discussing. For example, if we were reviewing a design proposal, the designer would share their mockups ahead of time, so we could come to the meeting with feedback ready. This not only saved time but also led to more thoughtful discussions. And because everyone knew what to expect, they were more engaged and less likely to tune out.

While agendas are essential for keeping meetings on track, they're not enough on their own. I've learned that the way you facilitate a meeting is just as important. On one project, I worked with a team where the loudest voices often dominated the conversation. This made it hard for quieter team members to contribute, and we ended up missing out on some great ideas. To address this, we started using **collaborative brainstorming tools** to level the playing field. For example, during one brainstorming session, we used a virtual whiteboard tool where everyone could add their ideas anonymously.

This encouraged participation from the entire team, not just the most vocal members. Once all the ideas were on the board, we grouped them into categories and discussed them as a team. This approach not only generated more ideas but also created a more inclusive environment where everyone felt heard.

Another tool that's been a game-changer for me is real-time collaboration software like Miro or Google Docs. On one project, we were tasked with coming up with a new feature for a mobile app. Instead of holding a traditional brainstorming session, we created a shared document where everyone could add their ideas over the course of a week. This gave people time to think and contribute at their own pace, rather than feeling pressured to come up with something on the spot. At the end of the week, we reviewed the document together and voted on the most promising ideas. This asynchronous approach worked particularly well for our team, as it allowed us to tap into everyone's creativity without the constraints of a scheduled meeting.

Of course, brainstorming is only the first step. To make meetings truly effective, you need to ensure that ideas and decisions are captured and acted upon. I've been in too many meetings where great ideas were discussed, but nothing came of them because no one took the time to document the outcomes. That's why I've made it a habit to always record **action items and outcomes** during meetings. On one project, I worked with a team that used a shared task management tool to track action items. During each meeting, we'd assign a note-taker to capture key decisions and next steps in the tool. For example, if we decided to implement a new feature, the note-taker would create a task with a clear description, a deadline, and an assignee. At the start of the next meeting, we'd review the action items to ensure they were completed. This simple practice kept us accountable and ensured that our meetings translated into real progress.

I've also found that summarizing the outcomes of a meeting is a great way to keep everyone aligned. On one project, I worked with a team where miscommunication was a frequent issue. We'd leave a meeting thinking we were all on the same page, only to realize later that we had different interpretations of what was decided. To address this, we started ending each meeting with a quick recap of the key takeaways. For example, the facilitator might say, "To summarize, we've decided to move forward with option A, and [name] will create a prototype by next Friday." This not only clarified the outcomes but also gave everyone a chance to raise any concerns before the meeting ended.

One of the most memorable examples of effective meeting practices came from a project where we were tasked with redesigning a company's internal tool. The project involved multiple stakeholders, including developers, designers, and business analysts, and it quickly became clear that we needed a better way to collaborate. We started by holding a kickoff meeting to align on goals and expectations. The agenda included topics like defining the project scope, identifying key stakeholders, and setting a timeline. During the meeting, we used a collaborative whiteboard tool to map out the user journey and identify pain points. By the end of the session, we had a clear plan for the next steps, and everyone felt invested in the project.

Throughout the project, we held regular brainstorming sessions to generate ideas and solve problems. One of the most productive sessions was when we were trying to come up with a new way to visualize data in the tool. Instead of starting with a blank slate, we used a collaborative tool to review examples of data visualizations from other products. This sparked a lively discussion, and we ended up combining elements from several examples to create a unique solution. After the session, we documented the ideas in a shared document and assigned action items to the team members responsible for implementing them.

At the end of each sprint, we held a retrospective meeting to reflect on what went well and what could be improved. These meetings were agenda-driven, with topics like "What worked well this sprint?" and "What challenges did we face?" We used a collaborative tool to collect feedback from the team, and we recorded action items to address any issues. For example, if someone mentioned that they were struggling with unclear requirements, we'd create an action item to improve the documentation for the next sprint. By continuously iterating on our processes, we were able to improve both our collaboration and our outcomes.

Looking back, I realize that effective meetings and brainstorming sessions aren't just about getting things done—they're about creating an environment where people feel empowered to contribute and collaborate. The agenda-driven meetings, the collaborative tools, the action items—each of these practices taught me something new about how to make the most of our time together. They taught me the importance of preparation, the value of inclusivity, and the power of accountability. But perhaps the most important lesson I've learned is that meetings aren't just a tool for communication—they're an opportunity to build trust, foster creativity, and move the team closer to its goals. And when you approach them with that mindset, they become not just productive, but transformative.

Sharing Knowledge and Continuous Learning

One of the most rewarding aspects of working in a team is the opportunity to learn from others. Early in my career, I thought I had to figure everything out on my own. I'd spend hours struggling with a problem, too embarrassed to ask for help, thinking it would make me look incompetent. But as I gained more experience, I realized that the best teams are those where knowledge flows freely, where people aren't afraid to ask questions, and where learning is a shared responsibility. Over the years, I've seen how practices like peer coding, mentorship, and knowledge-sharing sessions can transform a team—not just in terms of productivity, but in creating an environment where everyone feels supported and empowered to grow.

One of the most effective ways I've seen teams share knowledge is through peer coding and pair programming. I'll admit, I was skeptical of pair programming at first. The idea of sitting next to someone and coding together felt inefficient—wouldn't it be faster if we just worked on our own? But my perspective changed during a project where we were building a complex API for a financial services platform. The codebase was large and unfamiliar, and I was struggling to understand how everything fit together. One of my teammates suggested we pair program on a particularly tricky feature. At first, I was nervous—I didn't want to slow them down or make mistakes in front of them. But as we worked together, I realized how valuable the experience was. They pointed out patterns in the codebase that I hadn't noticed, explained design decisions that weren't documented, and helped me avoid pitfalls that would have taken me hours to debug on my own. By the end of the session, not only had we completed the feature, but I also had a much deeper understanding of the system.

Pair programming isn't just about solving problems—it's also a powerful way to share knowledge and build trust. On another project, I worked with a junior developer who was new to the team. They were talented but hesitant to ask questions, worried about appearing inexperienced. I suggested we pair program on a task, and during the session, I made a point to explain my thought process as we worked. For example, when we encountered a bug, I walked them through how I approached debugging, from reading error messages to tracing the flow of data through the code. I also encouraged them to take the keyboard and drive while I acted as a guide. By the end of the session, they not only felt more confident in their skills but also more comfortable asking for help in the future. That experience taught me that pair programming isn't just about writing code—it's about creating a space where people can learn from each other and grow together.

Another practice that's had a big impact on the teams I've worked with is lunch and learn sessions. These informal gatherings are a great way to share knowledge in a relaxed setting. On one project, we were working with a new framework that most of the team wasn't familiar with. To help everyone get up to speed, one of the developers who had experience with the framework offered to give a presentation during lunch. They walked us through the basics, shared tips and tricks they'd learned, and answered questions from the team. It was a low-pressure way to learn, and because it was during lunch, it didn't feel like an extra burden on anyone's schedule.

Over time, we started holding lunch and learn sessions regularly, covering a wide range of topics. For example, one session focused on best practices for writing unit tests, while another explored the principles of responsive design. These sessions weren't just about technical skills—they also gave us a chance to learn more about each other's interests and expertise. On one occasion, a teammate gave a presentation on accessibility in web design, a topic they were passionate about. Their enthusiasm was contagious, and it sparked a broader discussion about how we could make our products more inclusive. That session not only taught us something new but also strengthened our sense of shared purpose as a team.

One of the keys to successful lunch and learn sessions is making them inclusive and interactive. On one project, we had a session where a developer gave a live coding demonstration, walking us through how they built a feature from start to finish. They encouraged us to ask questions and suggest alternative approaches as they worked, which made the session feel more like a conversation than a lecture. Another time, we held a session where everyone brought a tip or trick they'd learned recently, whether it was a shortcut in their IDE or a new library they'd discovered. By the end of the session, we'd all learned something new, and it reinforced the idea that everyone has something valuable to contribute.

While practices like pair programming and lunch and learn sessions are great for sharing knowledge, I've found that the most impactful way to foster continuous learning is by creating a culture of mentorship. On one of my first teams, I had a mentor who made a huge difference in my development as a developer. They didn't just answer my questions—they took the time to understand my goals, gave me constructive feedback, and encouraged me to take on challenges that pushed me out of my comfort zone. For example, when I was hesitant to lead a code review, they encouraged me to give it a try and offered to review my comments before I shared them with the team. Their support gave me the confidence to step into a leadership role, and it's something I've tried to pay forward ever since.

Mentorship doesn't have to be formal to be effective. On one project, I worked with a senior developer who had a knack for teaching. Whenever we worked together, they'd take the time to explain not just what we were doing, but why. For example, when we were refactoring a piece of code, they explained the principles of clean code and how they applied to the changes we were making. They also encouraged me to ask questions and share my own ideas, even if I wasn't sure they were right. That experience taught me that mentorship isn't about having all the answers—it's about creating a space where people feel comfortable learning and growing.

As I've taken on more senior roles, I've tried to create that same kind of environment for others. On one team, we started a mentorship program where each new hire was paired with a more experienced team member. The mentor's role wasn't just to answer technical questions—it was also to help the new hire navigate the team's culture, build relationships, and set goals for their development. For example, one of the junior developers I mentored wanted to improve their public speaking skills. I encouraged them to give a presentation during a lunch and learn session, and I helped them prepare by reviewing their slides and giving them feedback on their delivery. Seeing their confidence grow over time was one of the most rewarding experiences of my career.

Fostering a culture of mentorship isn't just about supporting junior developers—it's about creating an environment where everyone feels empowered to learn and share their knowledge. On one project, we had a senior developer who was an expert in a particular technology but was less familiar with some of the newer tools we were using. During a pair programming session, a junior developer showed them a shortcut in the tool that saved them hours of work. That moment reinforced the idea that mentorship is a two-way street, and that everyone, regardless of their experience level, has something valuable to contribute.

Looking back, I realize that sharing knowledge and fostering continuous learning isn't just about improving technical skills—it's about building a team where people feel supported, valued, and inspired to grow. The pair programming sessions, the lunch and learns, the mentorship relationships—each of these practices taught me something new about what it means to collaborate and learn as a team. They taught me the importance of creating spaces where people feel safe to ask questions, the value of celebrating each other's expertise, and the power of investing in each other's growth. But perhaps the most important lesson I've learned is that learning isn't just an individual pursuit—it's a shared journey. And when a team commits to learning together, they don't just become better developers—they become better teammates, better problem-solvers, and better people.

CHAPTER ELEVEN

Scaling Your Application and Your Team

Scalability Fundamentals

When I first started working on web applications, scalability wasn't something I thought about much. My focus was on getting the application to work, not on how it would handle thousands—or even millions—of users. But that changed when I joined a team working on an e-commerce platform. The platform had been built quickly to meet the needs of a small customer base, but as the business grew, so did the traffic. What had once been a smooth-running application started to buckle under the pressure. Pages took forever to load, the database was constantly overloaded, and users were abandoning their carts in frustration. It was a wake-up call for me, and it taught me that scalability isn't just a technical challenge—it's a mindset that needs to be baked into your application from the start.

One of the first lessons I learned about scalability was the difference between horizontal and vertical scaling. At the time, our team's instinct was to throw more hardware at the problem. We upgraded the server to a more powerful machine with more CPU cores, more memory, and faster storage. This is what's known as vertical scaling—making a single machine bigger and more powerful. It worked, but only up to a point. As traffic continued to grow, we hit the limits of what even the most powerful server could handle. That's when we realized we needed to think differently.

Horizontal scaling, on the other hand, involves adding more machines to handle the load. Instead of relying on one massive server, you distribute the workload across multiple smaller servers. This approach is more complex to implement, but it's also much more flexible and cost-effective in the long run. For our e-commerce platform, we started by moving the application to a cloud provider that allowed us to spin up additional servers as needed. We set up an auto-scaling group that would automatically add or remove servers based on traffic. For example, during a big sale, when traffic spiked, the system would spin up additional servers to handle the load. Once the sale was over and traffic returned to normal, the extra servers would be shut down, saving us money. This experience taught me that while vertical scaling can be a quick fix, horizontal scaling is the key to building systems that can grow with your business.

Of course, horizontal scaling isn't just about adding more servers—it's also about distributing the workload effectively. That's where load balancing comes in. On the e-commerce platform, we used a load balancer to distribute incoming requests across our servers. This ensured that no single server was overwhelmed, and it also provided redundancy. If one server went down, the load balancer would automatically route traffic to the remaining servers, keeping the application online. Setting up the load balancer was relatively straightforward, but it had a huge impact on the reliability and performance of the platform.

Another technique that made a big difference was caching. One of the biggest bottlenecks in our application was the database. Every time a user loaded a product page, the application would query the database for the product details, the price, the inventory count, and so on. As traffic grew, these queries started to overwhelm the database, causing slowdowns and even crashes. To address this, we implemented a caching layer. Instead of querying the database for every request, the application would first check the cache. If the data was already in the cache, it could be served instantly, without hitting the database. For example, we cached the product details for popular items, which significantly reduced the load on the database and improved response times for users.

Caching isn't just about performance—it's also about cost. On another project, I worked with a team building a social media platform. One of the most expensive operations was generating the feed of posts for each user.

Initially, we generated the feed on the fly for every request, which required a lot of processing power. As the user base grew, this approach became unsustainable. To solve the problem, we started caching the feed for each user. Instead of generating the feed from scratch every time, we'd generate it once and store it in the cache. Subsequent requests could retrieve the cached feed, which was much faster and cheaper. This experience taught me that caching isn't just a technical optimization—it's a way to make your application more scalable and cost-efficient.

While techniques like load balancing and caching can help you scale a monolithic application, there comes a point where the monolith itself becomes a bottleneck. That's what happened on the e-commerce platform. The application was built as a single codebase, with all the functionality—product catalog, user accounts, checkout, and so on—tightly coupled together. As the team grew, it became harder to make changes without stepping on each other's toes. Deployments were risky because a bug in one part of the application could bring down the entire system. That's when we started exploring microservices as a way to scale both the application and the team.

The idea behind microservices is to break a monolithic application into smaller, independent services, each responsible for a specific piece of functionality. For example, on the e-commerce platform, we split the application into services for the product catalog, the shopping cart, the checkout process, and so on. Each service had its own codebase, its own database, and its own deployment pipeline. This approach had several advantages. First, it allowed us to scale each service independently. For example, during a big sale, the shopping cart service might need to handle a lot of traffic, while the user account service might not. With microservices, we could scale the shopping cart service without having to scale the entire application.

Second, microservices made it easier to develop and deploy new features. On the monolithic application, even a small change required testing and deploying the entire codebase, which was time-consuming and risky. With microservices, each service could be developed, tested, and deployed independently. For example, when we wanted to add a new payment method, we only needed to update the checkout service, without touching the rest of the application. This allowed us to move faster and reduce the risk of introducing bugs.

That's not to say that microservices are a silver bullet. They come with their own set of challenges, particularly around communication and coordination. On the e-commerce platform, we initially used REST APIs for communication between services. This worked well for simple interactions, but as the system grew, the number of API calls increased, which added latency and complexity. To address this, we started using a message queue to handle asynchronous communication between services. For example, when a user placed an order, the checkout service would publish a message to the queue, and the inventory service would consume the message to update the stock levels. This decoupled the services and made the system more resilient to failures.

Another challenge with microservices is managing data consistency. In a monolithic application, it's easy to enforce consistency because everything is in the same database. With microservices, each service has its own database, which can lead to inconsistencies if you're not careful. On the e-commerce platform, we ran into this issue when a user placed an order but the inventory service failed to update the stock levels. To solve this, we implemented a pattern called eventual consistency. Instead of trying to enforce consistency in real time, we allowed the system to reach a consistent state over time. For example, if the inventory update failed, the system would retry the operation until it succeeded. This approach required careful design, but it allowed us to build a scalable and reliable system.

Looking back, I realize that scalability isn't just about handling more traffic—it's about building systems that can grow and adapt as your needs change. The horizontal scaling, the load balancers, the caching layers, the microservices—each of these techniques taught me something new about what it takes to scale an application. They taught me the importance of thinking ahead, of designing systems that can handle not just today's challenges but tomorrow's as well. But perhaps the most important lesson I've learned is that scalability isn't just a technical problem—it's a team problem. And when you approach it with the right mindset, it becomes an opportunity to build not just better systems, but better teams.

Building a Resilient Team

Scaling an application is a technical challenge, but scaling a team is a human one. I learned this the hard way during a project where our team grew from five developers to over twenty in less than a year. At first, I was excited about the growth—it meant we had more resources to tackle the ambitious goals we'd set. But as the team expanded, so did the challenges. Communication became harder, processes that worked for a small team started to break down, and the quality of our work began to suffer. It was a humbling experience, but it taught me that building a resilient team isn't just about hiring more people—it's about hiring the right people, setting them up for success, and creating an environment where they can grow and thrive.

One of the most important lessons I've learned is that hiring the right talent is about more than just technical skills. Early in my career, I thought the best developers were the ones with the most impressive resumes or the deepest knowledge of a particular technology. But as I've been involved in more hiring decisions, I've come to realize that technical skills are only part of the equation. The best team members are those who not only have the skills to do the job but also the mindset to collaborate, learn, and adapt.

I remember one hiring process where we were looking for a senior developer to join our team. We interviewed a candidate who had an impressive background—they'd worked on high-profile projects and had deep expertise in the technologies we were using. But during the interview, it became clear that they weren't a good fit for our team. They dismissed other people's ideas, seemed unwilling to admit when they didn't know something, and didn't seem interested in mentoring junior developers. On paper, they were perfect, but we knew they wouldn't contribute to the kind of collaborative, supportive culture we were trying to build. We ended up hiring someone with less experience but a much better attitude, and it was one of the best decisions we made. That experience taught me that when you're hiring, you're not just looking for someone who can do the job—you're looking for someone who will make the team stronger.

Another lesson I've learned is the importance of tailoring the hiring process to identify the qualities you're looking for. On one project, we were building a team to work on a highly collaborative, fast-paced initiative. To find the right people, we designed an interview process that included a pair programming session. During the session, we weren't just looking at the candidate's coding skills—we were also paying attention to how they communicated, how they handled feedback, and how they approached problem-solving. For example, one candidate didn't solve the problem perfectly, but they asked thoughtful questions, explained their thought process clearly, and were open to suggestions. That told us they'd be a great collaborator, and they ended up being one of the most valuable members of the team.

Once you've hired the right people, the next challenge is setting them up for success. I've seen too many teams where new hires are thrown into the deep end with little guidance, expected to figure everything out on their own. This approach might work for some, but it often leads to frustration, mistakes, and even burnout. That's why I've come to appreciate the value of a strong onboarding process.

On one project, we had a new hire join the team just as we were in the middle of a major release. Everyone was so busy that we didn't take the time to onboard them properly. We gave them access to the codebase, pointed them to the documentation, and told them to start working on a feature. Unsurprisingly, they struggled. They didn't understand the architecture of the system, they weren't familiar with our coding standards, and they didn't know who to ask for help. It wasn't their fault—they were set up to fail. After that experience, we decided to overhaul our onboarding process.

The first thing we did was create a structured onboarding plan. For the first week, new hires would focus on getting familiar with the team, the tools, and the codebase. We assigned each new hire a mentor—someone they could go to with questions and who would guide them through their first few weeks. We also created a "starter project" for new hires to work on. This was a small, self-contained task that gave them a chance to learn the codebase and our processes without the pressure of working on a critical feature. For example, one new hire's starter project was to add a new filter to the search functionality. It was a relatively simple task, but it required them to touch several parts of the system, which gave them a good overview of how everything fit together. By the time they finished the project, they felt much more confident and prepared to take on more complex work.

Another thing we did was hold regular check-ins during the onboarding process. For example, at the end of the first week, we'd sit down with the new hire to see how they were doing, answer any questions, and get their feedback on the onboarding process. These check-ins weren't just about making sure they were on track—they were also an opportunity to show that we cared about their experience and wanted them to succeed. Over time, we found that this structured onboarding process not only helped new hires ramp up faster but also made them feel more connected to the team.

Of course, onboarding is just the beginning. To build a resilient team, you need to create an environment where people are constantly learning and growing. One of the best ways to do this is by encouraging skills development. On one project, we had a developer who was interested in learning more about DevOps. They didn't have much experience with it, but they were eager to learn. Instead of keeping them in their comfort zone, we encouraged them to take on a DevOps-related task—setting up a CI/CD pipeline for the project. We paired them with a more experienced team member who could guide them, and we gave them the time and resources they needed to learn. It took longer than if we'd assigned the task to someone with more experience, but it was worth it. Not only did they do a great job, but they also gained a new skill that made them an even more valuable member of the team.

Another way to encourage skills development is by creating opportunities for people to share what they've learned. On one team, we started holding "knowledge-sharing sessions" where team members could give short presentations on a topic they were passionate about. For example, one developer gave a talk on functional programming, while another shared tips for debugging performance issues. These sessions weren't just about learning new skills—they were also a way to celebrate each other's expertise and build a culture of continuous learning.

Mentorship is another powerful tool for skills development. On one project, I worked with a junior developer who was struggling with a particular task. Instead of just giving them the solution, I sat down with them and walked them through the problem, explaining my thought process and encouraging them to ask questions. It took longer than if I'd done it myself, but it was worth it. Not only did they learn how to solve that particular problem, but they also gained confidence in their ability to tackle similar challenges in the future. That experience taught me that mentorship isn't just about teaching skills—it's about empowering people to grow and succeed.

Looking back, I realize that building a resilient team isn't just about hiring talented people—it's about creating an environment where they can thrive. The hiring decisions, the onboarding processes, the skills development initiatives—each of these taught me something new about what it takes to build a strong team. They taught me the importance of looking beyond technical skills, of investing in people's growth, and of creating a culture where learning and collaboration are valued. But perhaps the most important lesson I've learned is that a resilient team isn't just a collection of individuals—it's a community. And when you invest in that community, you're not just building a team—you're building something that can weather any challenge and achieve great things together.

Orchestrating Growth

Scaling a team or an application is never just about adding more people or servers—it's about orchestrating growth in a way that doesn't compromise the culture, processes, or quality that made the team successful in the first place. I learned this lesson during a project where our team grew rapidly to meet the demands of a fast-scaling product. What started as a small, tight-knit group of developers quickly ballooned into a much larger team spread across multiple time zones. At first, we were excited about the growth—it meant we had the resources to tackle bigger challenges. But as the team expanded, we started to notice cracks in the foundation. Communication became harder, processes that worked for a small team started to break down, and the culture that had made the team so effective began to feel diluted. It was a challenging time, but it taught me that scaling isn't just about growth—it's about growing intentionally.

One of the first challenges we faced was scaling our culture and processes. When the team was small, we didn't need a lot of formal processes. Decisions were made quickly, everyone knew what everyone else was working on, and communication happened naturally. But as the team grew, that informal approach stopped working. For example, I remember a situation where two developers unknowingly worked on the same feature, duplicating each other's efforts. It wasn't anyone's fault—it was just a symptom of a growing team that lacked clear processes for coordination. To address this, we started holding regular planning meetings where we'd review the roadmap, assign tasks, and make sure everyone was aligned. At first, it felt like an unnecessary formality, but it quickly became clear how valuable it was. Not only did it prevent duplication of effort, but it also gave everyone a better understanding of how their work fit into the bigger picture.

Scaling culture, on the other hand, was a more subtle challenge. When the team was small, the culture was something we didn't have to think about—it just happened naturally. But as new people joined, we realized that if we didn't actively nurture the culture, it could easily get lost. For example, one of the things that made the team special was its emphasis on collaboration and learning. People weren't afraid to ask questions, share ideas, or admit when they didn't know something. But as the team grew, we noticed that some of the newer members were hesitant to speak up. They didn't feel as comfortable asking for help or challenging ideas, and it started to affect the team's dynamic. To address this, we made a conscious effort to reinforce the values that defined our culture. For example, during team meetings, we encouraged everyone to share their thoughts, even if they weren't sure they were "right." We also celebrated examples of collaboration and learning, like when someone helped a teammate solve a tricky problem or shared a new tool they'd discovered. Over time, these small actions helped to reinforce the culture and ensure that it scaled along with the team.

Another key to orchestrating growth is documentation and process standardization. When the team was small, we didn't need much documentation—if someone had a question, they could just ask the person sitting next to them. But as the team grew, that approach stopped working. For example, I remember a situation where a new hire spent hours trying to figure out how to set up their development environment because the instructions were scattered across multiple documents, some of which were outdated. It was a frustrating experience for them and a waste of time for the team. After that, we decided to invest in better documentation.

We started by creating a centralized knowledge base where all the team's documentation could live. This included everything from onboarding guides to coding standards to deployment processes. For example, we created a step-by-step guide for setting up the development environment, complete with screenshots and troubleshooting tips. We also documented our coding standards, including things like naming conventions, code review guidelines, and best practices for writing tests. This not only made it easier for new hires to get up to speed but also helped to ensure consistency across the codebase.

One of the most valuable things we did was to make documentation a team effort. Instead of relying on one person to write and maintain all the documentation, we encouraged everyone to contribute. For example, if someone discovered a new tool or process that made their work easier, they were encouraged to document it and share it with the team. We also made documentation part of our definition of "done" for tasks. For example, if someone implemented a new feature, they were responsible for updating the documentation to reflect any changes. This not only kept the documentation up to date but also reinforced the idea that documentation was a shared responsibility.

As the team grew, we also realized the importance of process standardization. When the team was small, everyone had their own way of doing things, and that was fine. But as the team grew, those differences started to create friction. For example, one developer might use a different branching strategy than the rest of the team, which could lead to merge conflicts and delays. To address this, we standardized our processes. For example, we adopted a consistent branching strategy (GitFlow) and created templates for things like pull requests and code reviews. We also standardized our deployment process, using a CI/CD pipeline to ensure that deployments were consistent and reliable. These changes took some time to implement, but they paid off in the long run by reducing friction and making the team more efficient.

One of the biggest challenges we faced as the team grew was handling distributed teams. At first, we were all in the same office, which made communication and collaboration easy. But as the team expanded, we started hiring people in different locations, and that introduced a whole new set of challenges. For example, I remember a situation where a developer in a different time zone was blocked on a task because they couldn't get an answer to a question. By the time someone responded, they'd already lost half a day of work. It was a frustrating experience for them and a reminder of how important it is to adapt your processes for a distributed team.

One of the first things we did was to adopt tools that made it easier to collaborate across locations. For example, we started using a project management tool to track tasks and progress, so everyone could see what was being worked on and who was responsible for what. We also started using a chat tool for real-time communication and a video conferencing tool for meetings. These tools helped to bridge the gap between locations and made it easier for the team to stay connected.

Another thing we did was to be more intentional about communication. For example, we made a point to document decisions and share them with the team, so everyone was on the same page. We also started holding regular "sync" meetings where team members could share updates, ask questions, and discuss any challenges they were facing. For example, during one sync meeting, a developer in a different location mentioned that they were struggling to understand a particular part of the codebase. This led to a discussion where the team shared tips and resources, and it ultimately helped them get unblocked.

One of the most valuable things we did was to create opportunities for the team to connect on a personal level. For example, we started holding virtual coffee chats where team members could get to know each other outside of work. We also organized an annual team retreat where everyone could meet in person, share ideas, and build relationships. These efforts helped to create a sense of connection and camaraderie, even for team members who were thousands of miles apart.

Looking back, I realize that orchestrating growth isn't just about scaling the team or the application—it's about scaling the culture, the processes, and the relationships that make the team successful. The planning meetings, the documentation, the virtual coffee chats—each of these taught me something new about what it takes to grow a team without losing what makes it special. They taught me the importance of being intentional, of investing in the team's success, and of creating an environment where everyone feels supported and connected. But perhaps the most important lesson I've learned is that growth isn't just about getting bigger—it's about getting better. And when you approach it with that mindset, you're not just scaling a team—you're building something that can thrive for years to come.

CHAPTER TWELVE

SECURITY BEST PRACTICES

Foundational Security Concepts

When I first started working as a developer, security wasn't something I thought about much. My focus was on building features, fixing bugs, and meeting deadlines. Security felt like someone else's responsibility—something for the IT team or the security experts to worry about. But that changed the day I was part of a team that experienced a security breach. It wasn't a massive, headline-grabbing incident, but it was enough to disrupt our work and shake our confidence. A vulnerability in our application allowed an attacker to access sensitive user data, and while we were able to fix the issue quickly, the damage was done. Users lost trust in our platform, and we spent weeks cleaning up the mess. That experience taught me that security isn't just a technical challenge—it's a fundamental part of building software that people can trust. And it starts with understanding the foundational concepts.

One of the first things I learned about security was the CIA Triad: Confidentiality, Integrity, and Availability. These three principles form the foundation of any secure system, and they're a useful framework for thinking about security holistically. I remember a project where we were building a healthcare application that stored sensitive patient data. Confidentiality was our top priority—we needed to ensure that only authorized users could access the data. To achieve this, we implemented strong authentication and encryption. For example, we used HTTPS to encrypt data in transit and AES encryption to protect data at rest. But confidentiality wasn't enough. We also needed to ensure the integrity of the data—that it couldn't be tampered with. To address this, we implemented checksums and digital signatures to detect any unauthorized changes. Finally, we had to think about availability. Even the most secure system is useless if it's not available when users need it. To ensure availability, we set up redundant servers and a robust backup system, so that even if one part of the system failed, the application would remain online. That project taught me that security isn't just about protecting data—it's about ensuring that the system works as intended, even in the face of threats.

Another important lesson I've learned is the importance of understanding common vulnerabilities. Early in my career, I worked on a project where we unknowingly introduced a SQL injection vulnerability. At the time, I didn't even know what SQL injection was. We had a search feature that allowed users to enter a query, and we passed the user input directly into a SQL statement without sanitizing it. It worked fine during testing, but when the application went live, an attacker used the vulnerability to access the database and extract sensitive information. It was a painful experience, but it taught me the importance of understanding the kinds of vulnerabilities attackers exploit.

One of the most valuable resources I've found for learning about vulnerabilities is the OWASP Top 10, a list of the most common security risks for web applications. For example, SQL injection, which I learned about the hard way, is one of the risks on the list. Another is cross-site scripting (XSS), where an attacker injects malicious scripts into a web page that's viewed by other users. I remember a project where we had a comment feature that allowed users to post text. We didn't sanitize the input properly, and an attacker was able to inject a script that stole users' session cookies. After that incident, we started using libraries to sanitize user input and implemented a content security policy (CSP) to prevent malicious scripts from running. These were relatively simple changes, but they made a huge difference in the security of the application.

Another risk on the OWASP Top 10 is broken authentication. On one project, we had a login system that used session IDs to keep users logged in. But we didn't implement proper session management, and an attacker was able to steal a session ID and impersonate another user. To fix the issue, we implemented secure cookies, set session timeouts, and added multi-factor authentication (MFA) for an extra layer of security. That experience taught me that authentication isn't just about verifying a user's identity—it's about ensuring that the system can't be easily tricked or bypassed.

While understanding vulnerabilities is important, it's just as important to design systems that minimize the risk of vulnerabilities in the first place. One of the most effective ways to do this is by following the principle of least privilege. This principle states that users and systems should only have the permissions they need to perform their tasks—nothing more. I first encountered this concept on a project where we were building an internal tool for a company. At the time, we gave every user full access to the database because it was easier than setting up granular permissions. But one day, a user accidentally deleted an entire table, causing a major disruption. It wasn't malicious—they just didn't realize the impact of what they were doing. After that incident, we implemented role-based access control (RBAC), where each user was assigned a role with specific permissions. For example, regular users could view data but not modify it, while administrators had more privileges. This not only reduced the risk of accidental damage but also made the system more secure against potential attackers.

The principle of least privilege doesn't just apply to users—it also applies to the system itself. On another project, we had a web server that ran with full administrative privileges. This wasn't a problem until the server was compromised, and the attacker was able to use the administrative privileges to take control of the entire system. After that, we started running the server with limited privileges, so that even if it was compromised, the attacker wouldn't have access to the rest of the system. We also implemented network segmentation, so that different parts of the system were isolated from each other. For example, the web server could only communicate with the application server, and the application server could only communicate with the database server. This made it much harder for an attacker to move laterally through the system.

One of the most memorable examples of the principle of least privilege came from a project where we were building a mobile app for a financial services company. The app needed to access sensitive user data, but we didn't want to store the data on the device, where it could be exposed if the device was lost or stolen. Instead, we designed the app to request the data from the server on an as-needed basis, and we used token-based authentication to ensure that only authorized requests were allowed. We also implemented fine-grained permissions, so that even if an attacker gained access to a user's account, they wouldn't be able to perform actions they weren't authorized for, like transferring money or changing account settings. This approach not only made the app more secure but also gave users peace of mind knowing that their data was protected.

Looking back, I realize that security isn't just about fixing vulnerabilities or implementing best practices—it's about adopting a mindset of vigilance and responsibility. The CIA Triad, the OWASP Top 10, the principle of least privilege—each of these taught me something new about what it takes to build secure systems. They taught me the importance of thinking ahead, of designing systems that are resilient to threats, and of constantly learning and adapting to new challenges. But perhaps the most important lesson I've learned is that security isn't just a technical problem—it's a human one. And when you approach it with that mindset, you're not just protecting your application—you're protecting the people who rely on it.

Secure Coding Techniques

When I first started writing code, I thought of security as something that came at the end of the development process. You'd build the application, test it, and then maybe run a security scan or two before deploying it. But over time, I learned that this approach is a recipe for disaster. Security isn't something you can bolt on at the last minute—it has to be baked into the code from the very beginning. I learned this lesson the hard way on a project where a seemingly small oversight in how we handled user input led to a major vulnerability. That experience taught me that secure coding isn't just about following best practices—it's about adopting a mindset where security is a priority at every step of the development process.

One of the first things I learned about secure coding was the importance of input validation and sanitization. Early in my career, I worked on a project where we built a web application with a search feature. Users could enter a query, and the application would search the database for matching results. It seemed simple enough, and we didn't think much about how we handled the user input. We passed the input directly into a SQL query, assuming that users would only enter valid search terms. But one day, someone entered a query that included a malicious SQL statement, and it caused the database to return sensitive information that should have been protected. That was my first encounter with SQL injection, and it was a wake-up call.

After that incident, I started learning about input validation and sanitization. Input validation is about ensuring that the data you receive is what you expect. For example, if a user is supposed to enter a number, you validate that the input is actually a number. If they're entering an email address, you check that it matches the format of a valid email. On the other hand, sanitization is about cleaning the input to remove any potentially harmful content. For example, if a user enters HTML or JavaScript into a text field, you sanitize the input to remove any tags or scripts that could be used for cross-site scripting (XSS) attacks.

On another project, we built a form where users could submit feedback. Initially, we didn't validate or sanitize the input, and it worked fine during testing. But when the application went live, someone submitted a feedback message that included a script to steal session cookies. It was a classic XSS attack, and it could have been easily prevented if we had sanitized the input. After that, we started using libraries like OWASP's ESAPI to sanitize user input and implemented a content security policy (CSP) to prevent malicious scripts from running. These changes weren't difficult to implement, but they made a huge difference in the security of the application.

Another critical aspect of secure coding is authentication and authorization. I've worked on several projects where we got these basics wrong, and the consequences were always painful. On one project, we built a login system that used session IDs to keep users logged in. But we didn't implement proper session management, and an attacker was able to steal a session ID and impersonate another user. It was a simple mistake, but it had serious consequences. After that, we started using secure cookies with the HttpOnly and Secure flags to protect session IDs, and we implemented session timeouts to reduce the risk of session hijacking.

Authentication is about verifying a user's identity, but authorization is about ensuring that users can only access the resources they're allowed to. I remember a project where we built an internal tool for a company. We assumed that because the tool was only accessible to employees, we didn't need to worry too much about authorization. But one day, we discovered that a regular employee was able to access an admin-only feature because we hadn't properly restricted access. It wasn't malicious—they were just curious—but it was a reminder of how important it is to enforce authorization at every level.

To address this, we implemented role-based access control (RBAC), where each user was assigned a role with specific permissions. For example, regular users could view data but not modify it, while administrators had more privileges. We also added checks at the API level to ensure that users couldn't access resources they weren't authorized for, even if they tried to bypass the front-end. These changes not only made the system more secure but also gave us peace of mind knowing that we had proper controls in place.

One of the most overlooked aspects of secure coding is secure logging and error handling. I learned this lesson on a project where we built an e-commerce platform. During testing, we noticed that some of the error messages included sensitive information, like database queries and stack traces. At first, we didn't think it was a big deal—after all, the error messages were only visible to us. But when the application went live, we forgot to disable the detailed error messages, and they ended up being exposed to users. This was a serious security risk because an attacker could use the information in the error messages to identify vulnerabilities in the system.

After that incident, we made a point to review our error handling practices. One of the first things we did was to ensure that error messages shown to users were generic and didn't reveal any sensitive information. For example, instead of displaying a detailed stack trace, we showed a simple message like "An error occurred. Please try again later." At the same time, we made sure that detailed error messages were logged securely so that developers could still debug issues without exposing sensitive information to users.

Logging is another area where security is often overlooked. On one project, we logged user activity to help with debugging and analytics. But we didn't think about the security implications of what we were logging. For example, we logged full credit card numbers and passwords in plain text, which was a major security risk. If an attacker had gained access to the logs, they would have had a treasure trove of sensitive information. After realizing our mistake, we started reviewing our logging practices to ensure that we weren't logging sensitive information unnecessarily. For example, instead of logging full credit card numbers, we only logged the last four digits. And instead of logging passwords, we logged a hash of the password. We also encrypted the logs and restricted access to them to ensure that only authorized users could view them.

One of the most valuable lessons I've learned about secure logging is the importance of balancing security with usability. On one project, we implemented such strict logging practices that it became difficult for developers to debug issues. For example, we redacted so much information from the logs that it was hard to figure out what was going wrong. To address this, we worked with the team to find a balance. We identified the information that was essential for debugging and made sure it was logged securely, while still redacting or encrypting sensitive information. This approach allowed us to maintain security without sacrificing usability.

Looking back, I realize that secure coding isn't just about following a checklist of best practices—it's about adopting a mindset where security is a priority at every step of the development process. The input validation, the authentication and authorization controls, the secure logging practices—each of these taught me something new about what it takes to build secure systems. They taught me the importance of thinking ahead, of designing systems that are resilient to threats, and of constantly learning and adapting to new challenges. But perhaps the most important lesson I've learned is that secure coding isn't just about protecting your application—it's about protecting the people who rely on it. And when you approach it with that mindset, you're not just writing code—you're building trust.

Applying Security Throughout Development

When I first started working on software projects, security felt like something that only came into play at the end of the development process. We'd build the application, test it for functionality, and then—if there was time—run a few security scans or ask someone from the security team to take a quick look. It wasn't until I was part of a project that suffered a major security incident that I realized how flawed this approach was. A vulnerability that could have been caught early in development ended up being exploited in production, and the fallout was painful. That experience taught me that security isn't something you can tack on at the end—it has to be integrated into every stage of the development process. From planning to deployment and beyond, security must be a constant consideration.

One of the most important lessons I've learned is the value of threat modeling and risk assessment early in the development process. I remember a project where we were building a financial application that handled sensitive user data, including bank account information. At the time, we were so focused on delivering features that we didn't stop to think about the potential threats to the system. It wasn't until a security consultant joined the project that we realized how vulnerable we were. The consultant introduced us to threat modeling, a process where you identify potential threats to your system, assess the risks, and design mitigations. It was an eye-opening experience.

We started by creating a diagram of the system architecture, including all the components and how they interacted. Then, we identified potential threats for each component. For example, we realized that the API endpoint for transferring funds could be a target for attackers trying to perform unauthorized transactions. We also identified risks like man-in-the-middle attacks on data in transit and brute-force attacks on user accounts. Once we had a list of threats, we assessed the likelihood and impact of each one. For example, a brute-force attack on user accounts was relatively likely, but the impact was limited because we had rate-limiting in place. On the other hand, a successful attack on the fund transfer endpoint could have catastrophic consequences, so we prioritized mitigating that risk.

The threat modeling process helped us design the system with security in mind. For example, we implemented strong authentication and authorization controls for the fund transfer endpoint, encrypted all data in transit using TLS, and added monitoring to detect suspicious activity. These measures weren't difficult to implement, but they made the system much more secure. That project taught me that threat modeling isn't just about identifying risks—it's about building a mindset where you're always thinking about how an attacker might exploit your system and how you can stop them.

Another critical part of applying security throughout development is code reviews with a security mindset. Early in my career, I thought of code reviews as a way to catch bugs and ensure code quality. Security wasn't something we explicitly looked for. But that changed when I worked on a project where a security vulnerability slipped through a code review and made it into production. The vulnerability was a simple one—a developer had used user input directly in a SQL query without sanitizing it, creating a SQL injection risk. It was an easy mistake to miss, but it could have been caught if we'd been reviewing the code with security in mind.

After that incident, we started incorporating security into our code review process. For example, we created a checklist of common security issues to look for during reviews, like improper input validation, hardcoded credentials, and insecure use of third-party libraries. We also encouraged reviewers to think like an attacker. For example, if a piece of code processed user input, we'd ask questions like, "What happens if the input is malicious? Could an attacker exploit this to gain access to the system?" This mindset shift made a big difference. On one project, a reviewer noticed that a piece of code was logging sensitive user data, which could have been a security risk if the logs were exposed. Because the reviewer was thinking about security, they flagged the issue, and we were able to fix it before it became a problem.

One of the most valuable things we did was to make security a shared responsibility. Instead of relying on a dedicated security team to catch vulnerabilities, we made it clear that everyone on the team was responsible for writing secure code and reviewing it for security issues. For example, we held training sessions where we taught developers about common vulnerabilities and how to avoid them. We also encouraged developers to share security tips and best practices during team meetings. Over time, this created a culture where security was a priority for everyone, not just an afterthought.

Of course, even with the best practices in place, vulnerabilities can still slip through. That's why it's so important to have a plan for monitoring, patching, and incident response. I learned this lesson on a project where we discovered a vulnerability in a third-party library we were using. The library was widely used and had been considered secure, but a researcher discovered a flaw that could allow an attacker to execute arbitrary code. The vulnerability was disclosed publicly, and we knew that attackers would start exploiting it soon. We had to act quickly to patch the vulnerability and protect our users.

The first step was to identify where the vulnerable library was being used in our system. This was easier said than done because we didn't have a complete inventory of our dependencies. After that incident, we started using tools to track our dependencies and monitor them for known vulnerabilities. For example, we integrated a dependency scanner into our CI/CD pipeline, so we'd be alerted if any of our libraries had security issues. This proactive approach helped us catch vulnerabilities early and patch them before they could be exploited.

Patching is only part of the equation—you also need to monitor your system for signs of an attack. On one project, we set up monitoring to detect unusual activity, like repeated failed login attempts or unexpected spikes in traffic. This helped us identify potential security incidents early and respond quickly. For example, we once noticed a sudden increase in failed login attempts from a single IP address. It turned out to be a brute-force attack, and we were able to block the IP before the attacker could gain access.

Incident response is another area where preparation is key. I remember a project where we didn't have a clear incident response plan, and it showed when we experienced a security breach. There was confusion about who was responsible for what, and it took longer than it should have to contain the breach and notify affected users. After that, we created an incident response plan that outlined the steps to take in the event of a security incident. For example, the plan included procedures for identifying and containing the breach, notifying stakeholders, and conducting a post-incident review to learn from the experience. We also held regular drills to practice the plan and ensure that everyone knew their role. This preparation paid off when we experienced another incident later on. Because we had a plan in place, we were able to respond quickly and minimize the impact.

Looking back, I realize that applying security throughout development isn't just about following best practices—it's about creating a culture where security is a priority at every stage of the process. The threat modeling sessions, the security-focused code reviews, the monitoring and incident response drills—each of these taught me something new about what it takes to build secure systems. They taught me the importance of thinking ahead, of being proactive rather than reactive, and of constantly learning and adapting to new challenges. But perhaps the most important lesson I've learned is that security isn't just a technical problem—it's a human one. And when you approach it with that mindset, you're not just building secure systems—you're building trust with the people who rely on them.

CHAPTER THIRTEEN

Quality Assurance and User Experience

Balancing Functionality with Usability

When I first started working as a developer, I was obsessed with functionality. My goal was to make things work—whether it was a feature, a button, or an entire application. If the code ran without errors and the feature did what it was supposed to, I considered it a success. But over time, I began to notice something: even when the functionality was flawless, users would still struggle. They'd get confused about how to use a feature, miss important buttons, or abandon the application altogether. It was frustrating because I thought I had done my job. But the truth was, I had only solved half the problem. Functionality is important, but it's not enough. If users can't figure out how to use your application—or if it doesn't meet their needs in a way that feels intuitive and accessible—then all the functionality in the world won't matter. That's when I realized the importance of balancing functionality with usability.

One of the most valuable lessons I've learned is the importance of usability testing and feedback loops. Early in my career, I worked on a project where we built a dashboard for a client to track their business metrics. The dashboard was packed with features: charts, filters, export options, and more. We were proud of what we had built, and we were confident the client would love it. But when we presented it to them, their reaction wasn't what we expected. They found the interface overwhelming and confusing. They couldn't figure out how to use some of the features, and they felt frustrated rather than empowered. It was a humbling experience, but it taught me an important lesson: just because something works doesn't mean it's usable.

After that, we started incorporating usability testing into our process. Instead of waiting until the end of the project to get feedback, we started testing early and often. For example, we'd create a prototype of a feature and ask users to try it out. We'd watch how they interacted with it, take note of where they got stuck, and ask for their feedback. I remember one test where we discovered that users were struggling to find a key feature because the button for it was buried in a dropdown menu. It was a simple fix—we moved the button to a more prominent location—but it made a huge difference in how users experienced the application.

One of the most important things I've learned about usability testing is the value of creating a feedback loop. It's not enough to test once and move on—you need to keep testing and iterating. On one project, we built a mobile app for a nonprofit organization. During the initial usability tests, we discovered that users were having trouble navigating the app. Based on their feedback, we made some changes to the navigation, but we didn't stop there. We tested the updated version with a new group of users, gathered more feedback, and made additional improvements. This iterative process helped us create an app that was not only functional but also intuitive and user-friendly.

Another critical aspect of balancing functionality with usability is accessibility considerations. I'll admit that when I first started developing software, accessibility wasn't something I thought about much. It wasn't that I didn't care—it just wasn't on my radar. But that changed when I worked on a project where accessibility was a top priority. We were building a web application for a government agency, and one of the requirements was that it had to meet WCAG (Web Content Accessibility Guidelines) standards. At first, I saw this as just another box to check. But as I started learning about accessibility, I realized how important it was—not just for people with disabilities, but for everyone.

One of the first things I learned was the importance of designing for screen readers. For example, we added descriptive alt text to all images, used semantic HTML to structure the content, and ensured that all interactive elements (like buttons and links) had clear labels. I remember testing the application with a screen reader for the first time and being amazed at how much of a difference these changes made. What had seemed like small details to me were actually critical for making the application usable for people who relied on assistive technologies.

Another lesson I learned was the importance of color contrast. On one project, we had designed a beautiful interface with soft pastel colors. It looked great, but during accessibility testing, we discovered that the text was hard to read for users with visual impairments. We adjusted the color palette to increase the contrast, and while it wasn't as visually striking, it was much more usable. That experience taught me that accessibility isn't about compromising on design—it's about creating a design that works for everyone.

Keyboard navigation is another area where accessibility often gets overlooked. On one project, we discovered that users who relied on keyboard navigation couldn't access some of the features because the focus order was inconsistent. For example, pressing the Tab key would skip over certain buttons or land on elements in an illogical order. We fixed this by ensuring that the focus order followed a logical sequence and by adding keyboard shortcuts for key actions. These changes didn't just benefit users with disabilities—they also made the application more efficient for power users who preferred using the keyboard over the mouse.

One of the most rewarding moments of my career came during a project where we built an e-learning platform. After launching the platform, we received an email from a user who was blind. They told us how much they appreciated the effort we had put into making the platform accessible and how it had allowed them to complete a course they wouldn't have been able to take otherwise. That email was a powerful reminder of why accessibility matters. It's not just about meeting requirements—it's about creating opportunities for everyone.

The final piece of the puzzle when it comes to balancing functionality with usability is cross-browser and cross-device testing. I learned this lesson the hard way on a project where we built a web application that worked perfectly in Chrome but was almost unusable in Internet Explorer. We didn't realize the problem until after the application went live, and by then, it was too late. Users were frustrated, and we had to scramble to fix the issues. That experience taught me that testing across different browsers and devices isn't optional—it's essential.

On one project, we built a responsive web application that needed to work on both desktop and mobile devices. During testing, we discovered that some of the features that worked perfectly on a desktop didn't translate well to mobile. For example, a drag-and-drop interface that was intuitive on a desktop was clunky and difficult to use on a touchscreen. We ended up redesigning the interface for mobile, using touch-friendly gestures instead of drag-and-drop. This wasn't something we had planned for initially, but it made a huge difference in the usability of the application.

Another challenge we faced was ensuring consistency across different browsers. On one project, we discovered that a CSS feature we were using wasn't supported in an older version of Safari, which caused the layout to break. To address this, we started using tools like BrowserStack to test the application in different browsers and on different devices. We also made a point to use progressive enhancement, where we built the application to work with basic functionality first and then added advanced features that would only load in modern browsers. This approach ensured that the application was usable for everyone, regardless of the browser or device they were using.

One of the most valuable lessons I've learned about cross-browser and cross-device testing is the importance of testing early and often. On one project, we waited until the end of development to start testing on different devices, and we ended up discovering a lot of issues that could have been caught earlier. After that, we started testing on multiple devices and browsers from the very beginning. For example, we'd test a new feature on a desktop browser, a mobile browser, and a tablet to make sure it worked consistently across all of them. This approach not only helped us catch issues early but also gave us confidence that the application would work for all users.

Looking back, I realize that balancing functionality with usability isn't just about following best practices—it's about putting yourself in the user's shoes. The usability tests, the accessibility improvements, the cross-browser testing—each of these taught me something new about what it takes to create an application that's not only functional but also intuitive, inclusive, and reliable. They taught me the importance of listening to users, of designing for everyone, and of constantly testing and iterating to make things better. But perhaps the most important lesson I've learned is that usability isn't just a feature—it's a fundamental part of what makes software successful. And when you approach it with that mindset, you're not just building an application—you're creating an experience that users will love.

The Role of QA in Development

When I first started working as a developer, I didn't fully understand the role of quality assurance (QA). To me, QA was just the team that tested the code after we were done building it. They'd find bugs, report them, and we'd fix them. It felt like a separate process, something that happened after the "real work" of development was finished. But as I gained more experience, I began to see how flawed that mindset was. QA isn't just about finding bugs—it's about ensuring that the software we build meets the needs of the users, works as intended, and delivers a great experience. And the more I worked with QA teams, the more I realized that they weren't just a safety net—they were an integral part of the development process.

One of the first lessons I learned was the difference between QA testing and developer testing. Early in my career, I worked on a project where the developers were responsible for testing their own code. At first, this seemed like a good idea. After all, who knows the code better than the person who wrote it? But it didn't take long for problems to arise. Developers, myself included, tended to focus on testing the "happy path"—the scenarios where everything works as expected. We'd run a few tests, confirm that the feature worked, and move on. But when the application went live, users started encountering issues we hadn't anticipated. They'd enter unexpected inputs, use features in ways we hadn't considered, or run into edge cases that we hadn't tested. It became clear that while developer testing was important, it wasn't enough.

That's where the QA team came in. Unlike developers, who are often focused on building features, QA professionals approach the software with a different mindset. They think like users, exploring the application from every angle and looking for ways it might break. I remember one project where a QA tester found a critical bug in a feature I had built. It was a subtle issue that only occurred when a user entered a specific combination of inputs, and I never would have thought to test for it. At first, I was frustrated—how had I missed this? But then I realized that this was exactly why we had a QA team. Their job wasn't to make me feel bad about my mistakes—it was to ensure that the software we delivered was as reliable and user-friendly as possible.

Over time, I came to appreciate the value of having both developer testing and QA testing. Developers are great at testing the functionality of the code they write, but QA brings a fresh perspective. They're not as close to the code, which allows them to approach it more objectively. They're also trained to think about edge cases, usability issues, and potential risks that developers might overlook. On one project, we implemented a process where developers would write unit tests and integration tests for their code, while the QA team focused on exploratory testing, usability testing, and end-to-end testing. This division of responsibilities allowed us to catch more issues and deliver a higher-quality product.

Another important lesson I've learned is the value of integrating QA early in the development process. On one project, we made the mistake of treating QA as a final step. We'd build the application, hand it off to the QA team, and wait for them to find bugs. But this approach created a lot of problems. For one thing, it slowed us down. If the QA team found a critical issue late in the process, we'd have to go back and make major changes, which often introduced new bugs. It also created a sense of separation between the developers and the QA team. We saw them as gatekeepers, and they saw us as the source of all the problems. It wasn't a healthy dynamic.

After that project, we decided to take a different approach. Instead of waiting until the end to involve QA, we started integrating them into the process from the very beginning. For example, during the planning phase, we'd invite QA team members to participate in discussions about the requirements and design. They'd ask questions like, "What happens if the user does this?" or "How will we handle this edge case?" These questions helped us think more critically about the features we were building and anticipate potential issues before we even wrote a line of code.

We also started involving QA during development. For example, on one project, we implemented a process where QA testers would review features as they were being built. If a developer finished a feature, they'd hand it off to QA for an initial round of testing before moving on to the next task. This allowed us to catch issues early, when they were easier and cheaper to fix. It also created a sense of collaboration between the developers and the QA team. Instead of working in silos, we were working together to build a better product.

One of the most valuable things we did was to create a shared understanding of quality. On one project, we held a workshop where developers and QA testers worked together to define what "quality" meant for our application. We talked about things like performance, usability, security, and reliability, and we came up with a set of criteria that we all agreed on. This shared understanding helped us align our efforts and work toward a common goal. It also helped us see QA as a partner, not an obstacle.

The final piece of the puzzle is continuous testing in CI/CD pipelines. I remember a project where we had a manual testing process. Every time we made a change to the code, we'd have to wait for the QA team to test it before we could deploy it. This created a bottleneck, especially as the project grew and the number of features increased. It also made it harder to catch issues early, because we weren't testing as frequently as we should have been.

To address this, we started automating our testing process and integrating it into our CI/CD pipeline. For example, we wrote automated tests for critical parts of the application, like the login system, the payment processing flow, and the API endpoints. Every time a developer pushed a change to the codebase, the CI/CD pipeline would run the tests automatically. If any of the tests failed, the pipeline would block the deployment and notify the team. This allowed us to catch issues early and fix them before they made it into production.

One of the most valuable things we did was to implement a mix of automated and manual testing. Automated tests were great for catching regressions and ensuring that the core functionality of the application worked as expected. But there were some things that automated tests couldn't catch, like usability issues or edge cases that required human intuition. That's where the QA team came in. They focused on exploratory testing, usability testing, and other areas where manual testing was more effective. This combination of automated and manual testing allowed us to deliver a high-quality product without slowing down the development process.

On one project, we also implemented a process called "shift-left testing," where we moved testing earlier in the development cycle. For example, instead of waiting until a feature was complete to test it, we'd write automated tests for the feature as it was being built. This allowed us to catch issues early and ensure that the feature was working as intended before it was even finished. It also gave developers more confidence in their code, because they knew it had been tested thoroughly.

Looking back, I realize that QA isn't just about finding bugs—it's about building confidence. The QA team, the automated tests, the early involvement in the process—all of these things helped us deliver software that we could be proud of. They taught me the importance of collaboration, of thinking critically about quality, and of constantly testing and iterating to make things better. But perhaps the most important lesson I've learned is that QA isn't just a step in the process—it's a mindset. And when you approach it with that mindset, you're not just building software—you're building trust with your users.

Crafting a Superb User Experience

When I first started working on user interfaces, I thought a good user experience (UX) was all about aesthetics. If the design looked sleek and modern, I assumed users would love it. But as I gained more experience, I realized that UX is about so much more than appearances. It's about how users feel when they interact with your product. It's about reducing frustration, making tasks easier, and creating an experience that feels intuitive and satisfying. I learned that good UX isn't just a design challenge—it's a psychological one. And the more I understood the psychology behind user behavior, the better I became at crafting experiences that truly resonated with users.

One of the most important lessons I've learned is the role of psychology in good UX. I remember working on a project where we built a task management app. The app was packed with features, but users weren't engaging with it the way we expected. They'd sign up, try it out for a few days, and then abandon it. We couldn't figure out why—after all, the app worked perfectly, and the design was visually appealing. It wasn't until we started talking to users that we realized the problem: the app felt overwhelming. There were too many features, too many options, and no clear path for getting started. Users didn't know where to begin, so they gave up.

That experience taught me the importance of understanding how users think and feel. For example, one psychological principle that's been incredibly useful is Hick's Law, which states that the more choices you present to a user, the longer it takes them to make a decision. In the task management app, we had overwhelmed users with too many options right from the start. To fix this, we simplified the onboarding process. Instead of showing users all the features at once, we guided them through a step-by-step tutorial that focused on the basics. We also added default settings and templates to help users get started quickly. These changes made the app feel less intimidating, and user engagement improved significantly.

Another psychological principle that's been invaluable is the concept of cognitive load. Users only have so much mental energy to spend on a task, and if your application requires too much effort to use, they'll get frustrated and leave. On one project, we built an e-commerce platform where users could customize their orders. The customization options were powerful, but the interface was cluttered and confusing. Users had to click through multiple menus and fill out long forms just to make a simple change. We realized that we were asking users to do too much, so we redesigned the interface to reduce cognitive load. For example, we grouped related options together, used visual cues to guide users, and added tooltips to explain complex features. These changes made the platform much easier to use, and sales increased as a result.

Another key aspect of crafting a superb user experience is simplifying workflows for users. I've worked on many projects where we focused so much on functionality that we forgot to think about how users would actually accomplish their tasks. One project that stands out was a customer support tool we built for a client. The tool had all the features the client wanted, but when we tested it with real users, we discovered that the workflows were unnecessarily complicated. For example, to resolve a support ticket, users had to navigate through multiple screens, copy and paste information between fields, and manually update the ticket status. It was tedious and time-consuming, and users were understandably frustrated.

To simplify the workflows, we started by mapping out the user journey. We looked at every step users had to take to complete a task and asked ourselves, "Is this step really necessary? Can we make it easier?" For example, instead of requiring users to copy and paste information, we added an auto-fill feature that pulled data from the system. We also consolidated multiple screens into a single, streamlined interface and added shortcuts for common actions. These changes dramatically reduced the time it took to resolve a ticket, and users were much happier as a result.

One of the most valuable things I've learned about simplifying workflows is the importance of observing users in action. On one project, we built a scheduling tool for a healthcare provider. During usability testing, we watched as users tried to schedule appointments. We noticed that they kept making the same mistakes, like clicking the wrong buttons or entering incorrect information. These weren't user errors—they were design flaws. For example, the "Save" and "Cancel" buttons were too close together, and the date picker was confusing to use. By observing users, we were able to identify these pain points and make changes to the design. For example, we added confirmation dialogs to prevent accidental cancellations and redesigned the date picker to make it more intuitive. These changes made the tool much easier to use and reduced the number of scheduling errors.

The final piece of the puzzle when it comes to crafting a superb user experience is leveraging analytics to refine UX. I used to think that once a feature was built and tested, the work was done. But I've since learned that UX is an ongoing process. No matter how much testing you do, you can't predict every way users will interact with your product. That's where analytics come in. By tracking how users actually use your application, you can identify areas for improvement and make data-driven decisions to refine the experience.

On one project, we built a mobile app for a fitness company. After the app launched, we noticed that users were abandoning the onboarding process at a specific step. At first, we weren't sure why, but when we looked at the analytics, we discovered that the step required users to enter a lot of personal information, like their weight, height, and fitness goals. It was too much to ask upfront, and users were dropping off as a result. To fix this, we simplified the onboarding process. Instead of asking for all the information at once, we broke it into smaller steps and made some of the questions optional. We also added a progress bar to show users how far along they were. These changes reduced the abandonment rate and helped more users complete the onboarding process.

Another way we've used analytics to refine UX is by tracking feature usage. On one project, we built a dashboard with a variety of widgets that users could customize. After the dashboard launched, we noticed that some widgets were rarely used, while others were extremely popular. Based on this data, we made changes to the default layout to highlight the most popular widgets and moved the less-used ones to a secondary menu. We also used the data to prioritize future development. For example, we added new features to the popular widgets and deprecated the ones that weren't being used. These changes helped us create a dashboard that better met the needs of our users.

One of the most important lessons I've learned about leveraging analytics is the value of combining quantitative and qualitative data. Analytics can tell you what users are doing, but they can't always tell you why. On one project, we noticed that users were spending a lot of time on a specific screen, but we weren't sure if that was a good thing or a bad thing. To find out, we conducted user interviews and discovered that the screen was confusing, and users were spending extra time trying to figure out how to complete their tasks. Based on this feedback, we redesigned the screen to make it more intuitive, and the time users spent on it decreased. This combination of analytics and user feedback allowed us to identify and address a problem we might have otherwise missed.

Looking back, I realize that crafting a superb user experience isn't just about following best practices—it's about understanding your users. The psychology of good UX, the simplified workflows, the data-driven refinements—each of these taught me something new about what it takes to create an experience that users love. They taught me the importance of listening to users, of observing their behavior, and of constantly iterating to make things better. But perhaps the most important lesson I've learned is that UX isn't just a feature—it's the foundation of a successful product. And when you approach it with that mindset, you're not just building software—you're creating an experience that users will remember.

CHAPTER FOURTEEN

MANAGING PROJECTS AND LEADERSHIP

Project Management Methodologies

When I first started working on software projects, I didn't think much about project management methodologies. To me, the process was simple: you'd get a list of requirements, build the features, and deliver the product. It wasn't until I worked on a project that spiraled out of control that I realized how important the right methodology is. The project started with a clear plan, but as requirements changed and deadlines slipped, we found ourselves scrambling to keep up. Communication broke down, priorities became unclear, and the team was frustrated. That experience taught me that project management isn't just about timelines and deliverables—it's about creating a structure that helps the team succeed, even when things don't go as planned.

One of the first things I learned about project management was the difference between Agile, Waterfall, and hybrid approaches. Early in my career, I worked on a project that followed the Waterfall methodology. The process was linear: we gathered all the requirements upfront, designed the system, built it, tested it, and then delivered it to the client. At first, this seemed like a logical approach. We had a clear plan, and everyone knew what they were supposed to do. But as the project progressed, we ran into problems. The client's needs changed, and because we had already completed the design phase, it was difficult to adapt. By the time we delivered the final product, it no longer met the client's expectations. It was a frustrating experience, but it taught me that while Waterfall works well for projects with stable requirements, it's not ideal for projects where things are likely to change.

After that, I worked on a project that used Agile, and it was a completely different experience. Instead of trying to plan everything upfront, we worked in short iterations called sprints. At the beginning of each sprint, we'd decide what features to work on, and at the end of the sprint, we'd deliver a working version of the product. This approach allowed us to adapt to changes quickly. For example, on one project, the client decided halfway through that they wanted to prioritize a new feature. Because we were working in sprints, we were able to adjust our priorities and deliver the feature without derailing the entire project. Agile also encouraged collaboration. We held daily stand-up meetings where everyone shared what they were working on, which helped us stay aligned and address issues quickly. That project taught me that Agile is a great choice for projects with evolving requirements, but it also requires a lot of discipline and communication to work effectively.

I've also worked on projects that used a hybrid approach, combining elements of both Waterfall and Agile. For example, on one project, we used Waterfall for the initial planning and design phases, where it was important to have a clear roadmap, and then switched to Agile for development and testing. This allowed us to start with a solid foundation while still being flexible enough to adapt to changes. One of the challenges of using a hybrid approach is finding the right balance. On one project, we spent too much time in the planning phase, which delayed the start of development. On another, we moved to Agile too quickly and ended up revisiting decisions we had made during the planning phase. Over time, I've learned that the key to a successful hybrid approach is to be intentional about which parts of the project use Waterfall and which use Agile, and to communicate clearly with the team about how the process will work.

Choosing the right methodology for a project isn't always straightforward. I've been on teams where we defaulted to Agile because it was trendy, even though it wasn't the best fit for the project. I've also seen teams stick with Waterfall because it was what they were used to, even when the project would have benefited from a more flexible approach. One of the most important lessons I've learned is that the right methodology depends on the needs of the project and the team. For example, on one project, we were building a mission-critical system for a government agency. The requirements were well-defined, and there was little room for error, so we chose Waterfall. On another project, we were building a mobile app for a startup, where the requirements were constantly changing based on user feedback. In that case, Agile was the better choice.

When choosing a methodology, it's also important to consider the team's experience and preferences. I remember one project where we tried to use Agile, but most of the team had only worked with Waterfall before. They struggled with the lack of a detailed plan and found the iterative process confusing. To address this, we held training sessions to help the team understand Agile principles and practices, and we started with a modified version of Agile that included more upfront planning. Over time, the team became more comfortable with the process, and we were able to transition to a more traditional Agile approach. That experience taught me that while it's important to choose the right methodology for the project, it's equally important to choose one that the team can execute effectively.

Once you've chosen a methodology, the next challenge is tracking progress and adapting quickly. On one project, we used a Kanban board to track our work. Each task was represented by a card, and the board had columns for "To Do," "In Progress," and "Done." As we worked on tasks, we moved the cards across the board. This simple system gave us a clear view of what everyone was working on and helped us identify bottlenecks. For example, at one point, we noticed that a lot of tasks were getting stuck in the "In Progress" column. When we looked closer, we realized that the team was taking on too many tasks at once and struggling to finish them. To address this, we limited the number of tasks that could be in progress at any given time, which helped the team focus and work more efficiently.

On another project, we used burndown charts to track our progress during sprints. A burndown chart shows how much work remains in a sprint and how quickly it's being completed. At the beginning of one sprint, we noticed that the chart was flat—no tasks were being completed. When we investigated, we discovered that the team was spending too much time on a single task that was more complex than we had anticipated. To address this, we broke the task into smaller, more manageable pieces and adjusted our priorities for the sprint. This allowed us to make progress and deliver value to the client, even though we didn't complete everything we had planned.

One of the most valuable lessons I've learned about tracking progress is the importance of regular check-ins. On one project, we held weekly retrospectives where the team reflected on what was working well and what could be improved. During one retrospective, a team member pointed out that our sprint goals were too ambitious, which was causing stress and leading to burnout. Based on this feedback, we started setting more realistic goals and focusing on delivering a smaller number of high-quality features. This not only improved the team's morale but also helped us deliver a better product.

Adapting quickly is another critical skill. On one project, we were building a web application for a client, and halfway through the project, they decided to change the scope. At first, the team was frustrated—we had already invested a lot of time in the original plan, and it felt like we were starting over. But instead of resisting the change, we worked with the client to reprioritize the features and adjust our timeline. We also held a team meeting to discuss the changes and make sure everyone was on the same page. By staying flexible and focusing on the client's needs, we were able to deliver a product that exceeded their expectations.

Looking back, I realize that project management methodologies aren't just about processes and tools—they're about people. The Waterfall plans, the Agile sprints, the hybrid approaches—each of these taught me something new about how to manage projects effectively. They taught me the importance of choosing the right methodology for the project and the team, of tracking progress and adapting quickly, and of creating a structure that helps the team succeed. But perhaps the most important lesson I've learned is that no methodology is perfect. The key is to stay flexible, listen to your team, and be willing to adapt as the project evolves. And when you approach project management with that mindset, you're not just managing tasks—you're leading a team to success.

Leadership in Technical Teams

When I first stepped into a leadership role, I thought being a leader meant having all the answers. I believed my job was to make decisions, solve problems, and guide the team toward success. But it didn't take long for me to realize how wrong I was. Leadership isn't about being the smartest person in the room or dictating what others should do—it's about empowering your team to do their best work. It's about creating an environment where people feel supported, valued, and inspired to contribute. This shift in perspective didn't happen overnight, but as I learned more about leadership, I discovered the power of servant leadership, the importance of mentoring, and the value of fostering innovation and collaboration.

One of the most transformative lessons I've learned is the importance of servant leadership principles. Early in my career, I worked under a manager who embodied this approach, though I didn't recognize it at the time. Instead of micromanaging or asserting authority, they focused on removing obstacles for the team. If someone was stuck on a problem, they'd step in—not to take over, but to provide guidance or connect them with the right resources. If a deadline was looming, they'd shield the team from unnecessary distractions so we could focus. They made it clear that their role wasn't to control us but to support us. At the time, I didn't fully appreciate how rare this kind of leadership was, but when I eventually found myself in a leadership position, I realized how much I had learned from their example.

I remember one project where I tried to apply these principles. We were building a complex API for a client, and the team was struggling with unclear requirements and tight deadlines. My instinct was to step in and start solving problems myself, but I knew that wouldn't help in the long run. Instead, I focused on creating an environment where the team could succeed. I scheduled a meeting with the client to clarify the requirements, then worked with the team to break the project into smaller, more manageable tasks. I also made sure everyone had the tools and resources they needed, whether that meant setting up a new testing environment or bringing in an expert to answer technical questions. By focusing on supporting the team rather than trying to control the process, I was able to help them deliver a high-quality product on time.

Servant leadership also means putting the needs of the team above your own ego. On one project, a junior developer came to me with an idea for improving our deployment process. At first, I was skeptical—it wasn't the way we'd always done things, and I wasn't sure it would work. But instead of dismissing the idea, I encouraged them to test it out. To my surprise, their approach not only worked but also saved us hours of manual effort. That experience taught me that good ideas can come from anyone, and as a leader, it's my job to create a culture where people feel comfortable sharing their ideas, even if they challenge the status quo.

Another critical aspect of leadership is mentoring junior developers. I've been fortunate to have mentors throughout my career who took the time to guide me, and I've tried to pay that forward by mentoring others. One of the most important things I've learned about mentoring is that it's not just about teaching technical skills—it's about helping people grow. I remember working with a junior developer who was struggling with imposter syndrome. They were talented and hardworking, but they doubted their abilities and were afraid to ask questions. I made a point to check in with them regularly, not just to review their work but to offer encouragement and remind them of their progress. I also shared stories about my own struggles early in my career, which helped them see that they weren't alone. Over time, their confidence grew, and they became one of the most valuable members of the team.

Mentoring also means giving people the opportunity to take on new challenges. On one project, I asked a junior developer to lead the implementation of a new feature. At first, they were hesitant—they didn't think they were ready, and they were afraid of making mistakes. But I assured them that I'd be there to support them and that mistakes were part of the learning process. They took on the challenge, and while there were a few bumps along the way, they did an excellent job. More importantly, the experience gave them the confidence to take on even bigger responsibilities in the future. That project taught me that one of the most important things a leader can do is to believe in their team, even when they don't yet believe in themselves.

Of course, mentoring isn't always easy. I've worked with junior developers who were resistant to feedback or who struggled to meet expectations. In those situations, I've found that the key is to approach the conversation with empathy and a focus on growth. For example, on one project, a junior developer was consistently missing deadlines. Instead of reprimanding them, I sat down with them to understand what was going on. It turned out that they were overwhelmed by the complexity of the tasks they'd been assigned. We worked together to break the tasks into smaller steps and set more realistic deadlines, and their performance improved significantly. That experience taught me that mentoring isn't about pushing people to meet your expectations—it's about helping them reach their potential.

Another essential part of leadership is driving innovation and collaboration. I've been on teams where innovation was stifled by a fear of failure or a rigid adherence to established processes. But I've also been on teams where innovation thrived because the leader created a culture of experimentation and collaboration. One of the most effective ways to drive innovation is to encourage the team to think creatively and take risks. On one project, we were tasked with improving the performance of a legacy system. The obvious solution was to optimize the existing code, but one of the developers suggested a more radical approach: rewriting the system using a modern framework. It was a risky idea, but after discussing the pros and cons as a team, we decided to give it a try. The rewrite wasn't without its challenges, but in the end, it resulted in a system that was not only faster but also easier to maintain. That project taught me that innovation often comes from challenging assumptions and being willing to take calculated risks.

Collaboration is another key ingredient for driving innovation. I've worked on projects where the team was divided into silos, with developers, designers, and QA working independently. This often led to miscommunication and missed opportunities for collaboration. On one project, we decided to take a different approach. Instead of working in silos, we held regular cross-functional meetings where everyone could share their ideas and provide feedback. For example, during one meeting, a QA tester pointed out a potential usability issue with a feature we were building. Their feedback led us to redesign the feature, which ultimately made it more user-friendly. That experience taught me that the best ideas often come from unexpected places, and as a leader, it's my job to create opportunities for collaboration.

One of the most rewarding aspects of driving innovation and collaboration is seeing the impact it has on the team. On one project, we held a hackathon where the team could work on any idea they wanted, as long as it was related to the project. The hackathon resulted in several innovative solutions, including a tool that automated a time-consuming part of our workflow. But more importantly, it brought the team closer together and created a sense of excitement and ownership. That experience taught me that innovation isn't just about coming up with new ideas—it's about creating a culture where people feel empowered to experiment, collaborate, and take pride in their work.

Looking back, I realize that leadership in technical teams isn't about having all the answers—it's about creating an environment where the team can thrive. The servant leadership principles, the mentoring relationships, the culture of innovation and collaboration—each of these taught me something new about what it means to be a leader. They taught me the importance of listening, of supporting the team, and of fostering a sense of trust and empowerment. But perhaps the most important lesson I've learned is that leadership isn't about you—it's about the people you lead. And when you approach leadership with that mindset, you're not just managing a team—you're inspiring them to achieve great things.

Stakeholder Management and Communication

When I first started managing projects, I underestimated how much of my time would be spent communicating with stakeholders. I thought the hard part of project management was building the product—writing code, solving technical challenges, and meeting deadlines. But I quickly learned that even the best technical work can fall apart if stakeholders aren't kept informed, expectations aren't managed, and risks aren't addressed. Stakeholder management isn't just about keeping people happy—it's about building trust, aligning goals, and ensuring that everyone involved in the project feels confident in its direction. Over the years, I've learned that clear communication, proactive risk management, and celebrating milestones are essential to successful stakeholder relationships.

One of the most important aspects of stakeholder management is delivering clear project updates. Early in my career, I worked on a project where communication with stakeholders was sporadic and inconsistent. We'd go weeks without providing updates, and when we did, they were filled with technical jargon that the stakeholders didn't understand. As a result, the stakeholders felt out of the loop, and their confidence in the project began to waver. I remember one particularly tense meeting where a stakeholder asked, "How do we know this is even on track?" That question hit me hard because I realized we hadn't done enough to keep them informed.

After that experience, I made it a priority to improve how I communicated project updates. On one project, I started sending out weekly status reports to the stakeholders. These reports were short and focused on what mattered most: what we had accomplished that week, what we were working on next, and any challenges or risks we were facing. I avoided technical jargon and used visuals like progress bars and charts to make the updates easier to understand. For example, if we were 60% done with a feature, I'd include a simple progress bar to show how far along we were. This approach not only kept the stakeholders informed but also gave them confidence that the project was moving in the right direction.

I also learned the importance of tailoring updates to the audience. On one project, we had two main groups of stakeholders: the technical team and the business team. The technical team wanted detailed updates about the architecture, performance, and code quality, while the business team cared more about timelines, budgets, and user impact. To address this, I created separate updates for each group, focusing on the information that was most relevant to them. This approach ensured that everyone got the information they needed without being overwhelmed by details they didn't care about.

Another key aspect of stakeholder management is managing expectations and risks. I've been on projects where expectations weren't clearly defined, and it always led to problems. On one project, the stakeholders expected a fully polished product by the end of the first phase, while the team was focused on delivering a minimum viable product (MVP). This misalignment caused frustration on both sides, and it wasn't until we sat down and clarified the goals that we were able to get back on track. That experience taught me that managing expectations starts with clear communication at the very beginning of the project. Before we write a single line of code, I make sure everyone understands what we're building, why we're building it, and what success looks like.

Managing expectations also means being honest about what's possible. On one project, a stakeholder asked for a new feature just a few weeks before the deadline. At first, I was tempted to say yes—I didn't want to disappoint them. But after discussing it with the team, it became clear that adding the feature would jeopardize the timeline and the quality of the product. Instead of overpromising, I explained the situation to the stakeholder and offered alternatives, like including the feature in a future release. While they were initially disappointed, they appreciated the honesty and the fact that we had a plan to address their request. That experience taught me that it's better to have a difficult conversation upfront than to overpromise and underdeliver.

Risk management is another critical part of managing expectations. I've worked on projects where risks were ignored until they became problems, and it always led to unnecessary stress and delays. On one project, we were building a web application with a tight deadline, and we knew from the start that integrating with a third-party API would be a challenge. Instead of waiting for the issue to arise, we flagged it as a risk during the planning phase and created a contingency plan. For example, we allocated extra time for the integration and identified alternative APIs we could use if the primary one didn't work out. When we did run into issues with the API, we were able to pivot quickly because we had already prepared for the possibility. That project taught me that proactive risk management isn't just about identifying potential problems—it's about having a plan to address them before they derail the project.

One of the most rewarding parts of stakeholder management is celebrating milestones and success. I've been on projects where we were so focused on the next deadline that we forgot to acknowledge what we had already accomplished. This can be demoralizing for the team and the stakeholders, especially on long projects where progress can feel slow. On one project, we were building a complex data analytics platform, and it took months before we had a working prototype. To keep the stakeholders engaged and the team motivated, we celebrated small milestones along the way. For example, when we completed the first module, we held a demo to showcase what we had built. The stakeholders were excited to see the progress, and the team felt a sense of accomplishment. These small celebrations helped build momentum and kept everyone focused on the end goal.

Celebrating milestones isn't just about boosting morale—it's also an opportunity to strengthen relationships with stakeholders. On one project, we delivered a major feature ahead of schedule, and the stakeholders were thrilled. To celebrate, we organized a small event where the team and the stakeholders could come together to reflect on the achievement. During the event, one of the stakeholders shared how the feature would make a difference for their users, and it was a powerful reminder of why we were doing the work. That experience taught me that celebrating success isn't just about recognizing the team's hard work—it's about connecting the work to its impact and reinforcing the shared purpose of the project.

Looking back, I realize that stakeholder management and communication are as much about relationships as they are about processes. The clear project updates, the honest conversations about expectations and risks, the celebrations of milestones—each of these taught me something new about what it takes to build trust and alignment with stakeholders. They taught me the importance of listening, of being transparent, and of creating a sense of shared ownership in the project. But perhaps the most important lesson I've learned is that stakeholder management isn't just a task on a checklist—it's an ongoing effort to ensure that everyone involved in the project feels informed, valued, and invested in its success. And when you approach it with that mindset, you're not just managing a project—you're building partnerships that can last far beyond the final deliverable.

CHAPTER FIFTEEN

Growing Your Career and Looking Ahead

Building a Professional Portfolio

When I first started my career as a developer, I didn't think much about building a professional portfolio. I assumed that my resume and technical skills would speak for themselves. But as I began applying for jobs and talking to other developers, I realized that a portfolio isn't just a collection of projects—it's a way to tell your story. It's a chance to show potential employers, collaborators, and clients not just what you've done, but how you think, solve problems, and approach your work. Over the years, I've learned that building a strong portfolio is one of the most important steps you can take to grow your career, and it's about more than just listing your accomplishments. It's about showcasing your projects, participating in the broader developer community, and crafting a personal brand that reflects who you are and what you stand for.

The first time I realized the power of a portfolio was when I applied for my first job out of college. I had a degree in computer science and a decent GPA, but so did most of the other candidates. What set me apart was a small web application I had built as a side project. It wasn't anything fancy—just a tool to help students organize their class schedules—but it demonstrated my ability to take an idea from concept to completion. During the interview, the hiring manager spent more time asking me about that project than anything else on my resume. They wanted to know how I came up with the idea, what challenges I faced, and how I solved them. That experience taught me that showcasing your projects isn't just about showing what you've built—it's about telling the story behind the work.

Over the years, I've worked on many projects, and I've learned that the best ones to include in your portfolio are those that demonstrate your skills, creativity, and problem-solving abilities. For example, on one project, I built a mobile app for a nonprofit organization that helped volunteers coordinate disaster relief efforts. The app wasn't just a technical challenge—it was an opportunity to make a real impact. When I included it in my portfolio, I didn't just describe the features of the app; I explained how I worked with the nonprofit to understand their needs, how I designed the user interface to be intuitive for volunteers in high-stress situations, and how I tested the app in the field to ensure it worked reliably. By focusing on the story behind the project, I was able to show not just what I built, but why it mattered.

Another way to build a strong portfolio is by participating in hackathons and contributing to open-source projects. I'll admit, the first time I attended a hackathon, I was intimidated. I didn't know what to expect, and I wasn't sure if I had the skills to keep up with the other participants. But I decided to give it a try, and it turned out to be one of the most rewarding experiences of my career. During the hackathon, I worked with a team to build a prototype for a smart home energy management system. We only had 24 hours, so we had to work quickly and make decisions on the fly. It was exhausting, but it was also exhilarating. At the end of the hackathon, we presented our prototype to a panel of judges, and while we didn't win, the experience taught me a lot about teamwork, problem-solving, and working under pressure.

Hackathons are a great way to build your portfolio because they give you the opportunity to work on unique, creative projects that you might not encounter in your day-to-day work. They also show potential employers that you're passionate about your craft and willing to push yourself outside your comfort zone. For example, one of my friends landed a job at a top tech company because of a project they built during a hackathon. The project was a machine learning tool that analyzed social media data to predict trends, and it caught the attention of a recruiter who was impressed by their initiative and creativity. That story reinforced for me the value of hackathons—not just as a learning experience, but as a way to stand out in a competitive job market.

Contributing to open-source projects is another excellent way to build your portfolio. I remember the first time I submitted a pull request to an open-source project. It was a small bug fix, but I was nervous. I wasn't sure if my code would be good enough, and I worried about how the maintainers would respond. But to my surprise, they were incredibly welcoming. They reviewed my code, provided constructive feedback, and thanked me for my contribution. That experience gave me the confidence to take on more significant contributions, and over time, I became a regular contributor to several projects.

Open-source contributions are valuable for your portfolio because they demonstrate your ability to collaborate with others, work with existing codebases, and contribute to the broader developer community. They also give you the opportunity to work on projects that have real-world impact. For example, one of the open-source projects I contributed to was a library for building accessible web applications. Knowing that my work was helping make the web more inclusive was incredibly rewarding, and it was something I was proud to include in my portfolio. When I talked about it during job interviews, it showed not just my technical skills, but also my values and commitment to making a difference.

While showcasing your projects and participating in the developer community are important, building a professional portfolio is also about crafting a personal brand. Early in my career, I didn't think much about my personal brand. I thought it was something only entrepreneurs or influencers needed to worry about. But as I started networking and applying for jobs, I realized that your personal brand is simply how you present yourself to the world. It's about showing who you are, what you stand for, and what makes you unique.

One of the first steps I took to craft my personal brand was creating a personal website. At first, I wasn't sure what to include, but I decided to focus on three things: my projects, my blog, and my contact information. For my projects, I included detailed case studies that explained not just what I built, but how I approached the work and what I learned. For my blog, I wrote about topics I was passionate about, like accessibility in web design and the importance of testing. And for my contact information, I made it easy for people to reach out to me, whether they wanted to collaborate on a project or just connect.

Over time, I've learned that crafting a personal brand is about more than just having a website—it's about being intentional about how you present yourself online and in person. For example, I've made a point to be active on platforms like GitHub, LinkedIn, and Twitter, where I can share my work, connect with other developers, and contribute to discussions about technology. I've also given talks at meetups and conferences, which has helped me build my reputation as someone who's knowledgeable and passionate about my field. One of the most rewarding moments of my career was when someone approached me after a talk and said, "I've been following your work for a while, and it's inspired me to start learning web development." That experience reminded me that your personal brand isn't just about advancing your career—it's about sharing your knowledge and inspiring others.

Looking back, I realize that building a professional portfolio isn't just about showcasing your skills—it's about telling your story. The projects you include, the hackathons you participate in, the open-source contributions you make, and the personal brand you craft—all of these are opportunities to show not just what you've done, but who you are and what you stand for. They're opportunities to connect with others, to make an impact, and to grow as a developer and as a person. And when you approach your portfolio with that mindset, it becomes more than just a collection of work—it becomes a reflection of your journey and a foundation for your future.

Opportunities for Continuous Growth

When I first started my career, I thought growth was something that happened naturally. I assumed that as long as I kept working hard and learning on the job, I'd continue to improve. But as I gained more experience, I realized that growth doesn't just happen—you have to seek it out. The most successful people I've met in the tech industry didn't just rely on their day-to-day work to develop their skills. They actively pursued opportunities to learn, connect, and challenge themselves. Whether it's attending conferences, earning certifications, or building a strong professional network, continuous growth is about being intentional and proactive in shaping your career.

One of the most impactful ways I've found to grow is by attending conferences and meetups. Early in my career, I was hesitant to attend these events. I wasn't sure if I'd fit in, and I worried that I didn't have enough experience to contribute to the conversations. But a colleague convinced me to attend a local developer meetup, and it turned out to be a turning point in my career. The meetup was small and informal, but it gave me the chance to hear from other developers about the challenges they were facing and the solutions they were exploring. I left the event feeling inspired and energized, and I realized how valuable it was to step outside my own bubble and learn from others.

Over time, I started attending larger conferences, and the benefits only grew. At one conference, I attended a talk on performance optimization for web applications. The speaker shared practical techniques for improving load times, and I immediately saw how I could apply those techniques to a project I was working on. But the real value came after the talk, when I had the chance to chat with the speaker and ask questions about some of the specific challenges I was facing. That conversation not only helped me solve a tricky problem, but it also gave me a new perspective on how to approach performance optimization in general. Experiences like that have taught me that conferences aren't just about listening to talks—they're about connecting with people who can inspire and challenge you.

Meetups, on the other hand, have been a great way to build relationships with local developers. On one occasion, I attended a meetup focused on open-source contributions. During the event, I met a developer who was working on a project that aligned with my interests, and we ended up collaborating on a feature together. That collaboration not only helped me improve my skills, but it also led to a lasting professional relationship. We've stayed in touch over the years, and they've even referred me to opportunities that I wouldn't have found on my own. That experience taught me that meetups aren't just about learning—they're about building connections that can support your growth in unexpected ways.

Another way to invest in your growth is by seeking certifications and advanced degrees. I'll admit, I was skeptical about certifications at first. I thought they were just pieces of paper that didn't really prove anything. But when I started working on a project that required deep knowledge of cloud computing, I realized how valuable certifications could be. I decided to pursue a certification in cloud architecture, and the process of studying for the exam forced me to dive deep into topics I hadn't encountered before. By the time I earned the certification, I not only had a better understanding of cloud computing, but I also had a credential that demonstrated my expertise to potential employers and clients.

Certifications can be especially valuable if you're looking to specialize in a particular area. For example, one of my colleagues wanted to transition from general software development to cybersecurity. They decided to pursue a certification in ethical hacking, and the process not only gave them the skills they needed but also helped them stand out in a competitive job market. When they applied for a cybersecurity role, the certification showed that they were serious about the field and had the knowledge to back it up. That experience taught me that certifications aren't just about learning—they're about signaling your expertise and commitment to a particular area.

Advanced degrees, on the other hand, can be a more significant investment, but they can also open doors that might otherwise be closed. I've worked with developers who pursued master's degrees in computer science, data science, or business administration, and each of them had a different reason for doing so. One developer wanted to deepen their technical knowledge and transition into a research role, while another wanted to gain the business skills needed to move into a leadership position. In both cases, the advanced degree gave them the tools and credentials they needed to achieve their goals. That said, I've also seen people succeed without advanced degrees, so it's important to weigh the costs and benefits and decide what's right for you.

For me, the most valuable part of pursuing certifications and advanced degrees has been the opportunity to learn from others. When I was studying for my cloud architecture certification, I joined an online study group where people shared resources, asked questions, and supported each other. That group not only helped me pass the exam, but it also introduced me to a community of like-minded professionals who were passionate about cloud computing. Similarly, when a friend pursued a master's degree in data science, they found that the relationships they built with their professors and classmates were just as valuable as the knowledge they gained. Those experiences have taught me that learning is rarely a solo endeavor—it's something that happens best when you're part of a community.

Speaking of community, one of the most important ways to grow is by building networks and collaborations. Early in my career, I didn't think much about networking. I assumed that as long as I did good work, opportunities would come to me. But as I started meeting more people in the industry, I realized how much of a difference a strong network can make. Networking isn't just about finding jobs—it's about learning from others, sharing ideas, and building relationships that can support you throughout your career.

One of the most valuable networking experiences I've had was at a conference where I met a developer who was working on a project similar to one I had just completed. We started talking about the challenges we had faced and the solutions we had tried, and by the end of the conversation, we had exchanged contact information and agreed to stay in touch. A few months later, they reached out to me with a question about a problem they were facing, and I was able to help them find a solution. That interaction not only strengthened our relationship, but it also gave me a new perspective on the problem I had faced in my own project. That experience taught me that networking isn't just about what you can get—it's about what you can give.

Collaboration is another powerful way to grow. On one project, I worked with a team of developers from different companies to build an open-source tool for data visualization. The project was challenging, but it was also incredibly rewarding. Each member of the team brought their own expertise and perspective, and I learned a lot from seeing how they approached problems. For example, one developer had a background in design, and they taught me how to think about user experience in a way I hadn't considered before. That collaboration not only improved my technical skills, but it also gave me a deeper appreciation for the value of diverse perspectives.

Building networks and collaborations doesn't have to be formal or intimidating. Some of the most valuable connections I've made have come from casual conversations at meetups, conferences, or even online forums. For example, I once posted a question on a developer forum about a problem I was facing, and someone responded with a detailed explanation that helped me solve it. We ended up connecting on LinkedIn, and over time, we've exchanged ideas and resources that have helped both of us grow. That experience taught me that networking isn't about collecting business cards or making small talk—it's about building genuine relationships based on shared interests and mutual support.

Looking back, I realize that continuous growth isn't just about learning new skills—it's about seeking out opportunities to challenge yourself, connect with others, and expand your horizons. The conferences, certifications, and collaborations I've pursued have taught me that growth doesn't happen in isolation—it happens when you're part of a community that inspires and supports you. And when you approach growth with that mindset, it becomes more than just a way to advance your career—it becomes a way to enrich your life and make a meaningful impact on the world around you.

Future Trends and Final Takeaways

When I think about the future of technology, I'm reminded of a conversation I had with a mentor early in my career. I was just starting out as a developer, and I asked them what they thought the most important skill for a successful career was. I expected them to say something technical, like mastering a specific programming language or framework. Instead, they said, "The most important skill is adaptability. Technology changes so fast that the tools you're using today might be obsolete in five years. If you can't adapt, you'll get left behind." At the time, I didn't fully understand what they meant, but as I've watched the industry evolve, their words have stuck with me. The rise of emerging technologies like artificial intelligence, blockchain, and quantum computing has made it clear that staying relevant in this field requires more than just technical expertise—it requires a commitment to lifelong learning and a willingness to embrace change.

One of the most exciting aspects of working in tech is the constant emergence of new technologies. I remember the first time I worked on a project that used artificial intelligence (AI). It was a chatbot for a customer support system, and while the technology was still relatively new, it was clear that AI had the potential to transform the way we interact with software. At first, I was intimidated by the complexity of machine learning algorithms and neural networks, but as I started learning more about the field, I realized that you don't have to be an expert in AI to start using it. There are plenty of tools and frameworks, like TensorFlow and PyTorch, that make it accessible even to developers who are new to the field. That project taught me that emerging technologies often seem daunting at first, but with the right mindset and resources, they can open up incredible opportunities.

Blockchain is another technology that has captured my attention in recent years. I'll admit, when I first heard about blockchain, I thought it was just about cryptocurrencies like Bitcoin. But as I started exploring the technology, I realized that its potential goes far beyond digital currencies. For example, I worked on a project for a supply chain company that wanted to use blockchain to improve transparency and traceability. By creating a decentralized ledger, we were able to track the movement of goods from the manufacturer to the retailer, ensuring that every step of the process was recorded and verifiable. That experience taught me that blockchain isn't just a buzzword—it's a tool that can solve real-world problems in innovative ways.

Of course, not every emerging technology will become the next big thing. I've seen plenty of trends come and go, and it can be hard to know which ones are worth investing your time in. One of the strategies I've found helpful is to focus on the problems a technology is trying to solve rather than the technology itself. For example, AI and blockchain are both tools for solving specific types of problems—AI excels at automating tasks and making predictions, while blockchain is great for creating trust in decentralized systems. By understanding the problems these technologies address, you can better evaluate whether they're relevant to your work and how you might use them.

Staying relevant in a rapidly changing industry isn't just about learning new technologies—it's about staying curious and open to change. I've worked with developers who were resistant to learning new tools because they were comfortable with the ones they already knew. While there's nothing wrong with having a favorite language or framework, I've learned that clinging too tightly to what you know can hold you back. On one project, I was asked to use a new front-end framework that I wasn't familiar with. My first instinct was to push back—I was already comfortable with the framework I had been using, and I didn't see the need to switch. But as I started working with the new framework, I realized that it had features that made the development process faster and more efficient. That experience taught me that staying relevant means being willing to step outside your comfort zone and try new things, even if it feels uncomfortable at first.

One of the best ways to stay relevant is to surround yourself with people who are passionate about learning. I've been fortunate to work on teams where knowledge-sharing was a core part of the culture. On one team, we held regular "tech talks" where team members could share what they were learning, whether it was a new programming language, a design pattern, or a tool they had discovered. These talks not only helped us stay up-to-date with the latest trends, but they also created a sense of camaraderie and mutual support. For example, one of my colleagues gave a talk on serverless architecture, which was a relatively new concept at the time. Their presentation sparked a discussion about how we could use serverless technologies in our own projects, and it ultimately led to us adopting a more scalable and cost-effective approach to building our applications. That experience taught me that staying relevant isn't just about individual effort—it's about being part of a community that values learning and growth.

As the industry continues to evolve, one thing has become clear to me: lifelong learning isn't optional—it's essential. I've seen developers who stopped learning after they mastered a particular technology, and over time, they found themselves struggling to keep up as the industry moved on. On the other hand, I've also seen developers who embraced lifelong learning and thrived, even as the tools and technologies around them changed. One of the most inspiring examples I've seen is a senior developer I worked with who had been in the industry for over 20 years. Despite their experience, they were always eager to learn new things. I remember them taking an online course on machine learning because they wanted to understand how it could be applied to our projects. Their curiosity and humility were a reminder that no matter how experienced you are, there's always more to learn.

For me, embracing lifelong learning has meant making it a regular part of my routine. I set aside time each week to read articles, watch tutorials, or work on side projects that challenge me to learn something new. For example, when I wanted to learn more about AI, I started by taking an online course that covered the basics of machine learning. From there, I built a small project—a recommendation system for a movie database—that allowed me to apply what I had learned in a practical way. That project not only deepened my understanding of AI but also gave me something to showcase in my portfolio. Experiences like that have taught me that learning is most effective when it's hands-on and tied to real-world problems.

Another important aspect of lifelong learning is being willing to unlearn old habits and adapt to new ways of thinking. I've worked on projects where the team was using outdated practices because "that's the way we've always done it." While it can be tempting to stick with what's familiar, I've learned that growth often requires letting go of old assumptions and embracing new approaches. For example, on one project, we transitioned from a monolithic architecture to a microservices-based approach. At first, the change was challenging—many of us were used to working with monoliths, and we had to learn new tools and patterns to make the transition. But over time, we saw the benefits of the new approach, and it made us more open to trying new things in the future. That experience taught me that lifelong learning isn't just about acquiring new knowledge—it's about being willing to evolve and adapt.

Looking ahead, I'm excited about the possibilities that emerging technologies and lifelong learning can bring. The rise of AI, blockchain, and other innovations has shown me that the future of technology is full of opportunities for those who are willing to embrace change and keep learning. But perhaps the most important lesson I've learned is that growth isn't just about staying relevant—it's about finding joy and fulfillment in the process of learning and creating. Whether it's building a new project, exploring a new technology, or collaborating with others, the journey of growth is what makes a career in tech so rewarding. And as I look to the future, I'm reminded of what my mentor told me all those years ago: adaptability is the key to success. By staying curious, open, and committed to lifelong learning, we can not only keep up with the changes in the industry but also shape the future of technology in meaningful ways.

End Notes

This book would not have been possible without the support and encouragement of many people. To my family and friends, thank you for your patience and belief in me throughout this journey. To my mentors, colleagues, and the developer community, your insights and shared experiences have been invaluable in shaping the ideas presented here. And to my readers, thank you for taking the time to explore this philosophy of thoughtful development. Your passion for growth and learning inspires me every day.

Appendix

A. Key Takeaways

- Thoughtful development is about planning, executing, and reflecting with intention.
- Slowing down to think thrice before coding once leads to better results, fewer bugs, and happier clients.
- Collaboration, communication, and continuous learning are essential for success in software development.

B. Tools and Resources

- Project Management Tools: Trello, Jira, Asana
- Prototyping Tools: Figma, Adobe XD, Sketch
- Code Quality Tools: SonarQube, ESLint, Prettier
- Version Control: Git, GitHub, GitLab
- Learning Resources:

  - Clean Code by Robert C. Martin
  - The Pragmatic Programmer by Andrew Hunt and David Thomas
  - Online platforms: Pluralsight, Udemy, freeCodeCamp

Glossary

A quick reference for key terms used in the book:

- Thoughtful Development: A mindset and approach to software development that emphasizes planning, execution, and reflection.
- Design Thinking: A problem-solving approach that focuses on empathy, ideation, and iteration.
- Technical Debt: The cost of shortcuts taken during development that may require rework in the future.
- Scalability: The ability of a system to handle increased workload or growth without performance degradation.

References

- A list of references and further reading materials:
- Martin, Robert C. Clean Code: A Handbook of Agile Software Craftsmanship.
- Hunt, Andrew, and Thomas, David. The Pragmatic Programmer: Your Journey to Mastery.
- Dweck, Carol S. Mindset: The New Psychology of Success.
- Beck, Kent. Test-Driven Development: By Example.
- Ries, Eric. The Lean Startup: How Today's Entrepreneurs Use Continuous Innovation to Create Radically Successful Businesses.

About the Author

Amit Gujrathi is a software developer, writer, and advocate for thoughtful development practices. With years of experience in the tech industry, Amit has worked on a wide range of projects, from small startups to large-scale enterprise systems. Passionate about clean code, collaboration, and continuous learning, Amit believes that great software is built not just with skill but with intention and care.

Call to Action

Thank you for reading "Think Thrice, Code Once"! If you found this book helpful, I'd love to hear your thoughts. Please consider leaving a review or sharing your feedback on [platform, e.g., Amazon, Goodreads, or your website]. Your support helps spread the message of thoughtful development to more developers around the world.

Stay connected!

END NOTES

162

9 7988 96 99 6651